LIVING OVERSEAS BO

To: Our readers
From: Robert Johnston
Re: A toast to the adventurous among us!

The trend for U.S. and Canadian citizens to step across the border to Mexico seeking living and small business opportunities has accelerated at a dizzying pace over the past year.

Some are young people fresh out of college, like Katie Reeder, who "just didn't like any of the opportunities out there," so she ventured down to Mexico and now owns a successful export firm. Others are akin to Rod Collins who found he just had "a better lifestyle" here [Mexico] than in the states. Many retirees can relate to part-time resident William Cox who found "wintering" in Mexico gave him the retirement life he dreamed of while escaping Chicago's harsh winters.

To these adventurous expats and all the others who've proved you can go international, regardless of experience or size of your bank account, and to the ones planning to take the step, I salute you.

Robert Johnston
Living Overseas Books

DON'T MISS THESE OTHER LIVING OVERSEAS BOOKS

Costa Rica

Mexico

Belize

Dominican Republic

Living Overseas: What You Need to Know

Living Overseas

MEXICO

Living Overseas Books

Naples, Florida

TO THE PEOPLE OF MEXICO

Living Oveseas Books
P.O. Box 9481
Naples, Florida 34101
www.livingoverseas.com
robert@livingoverseas.com

This book would not have been possible without
the valuable help from various Mexican consulates and
numerous overseas experts in law, accounting,
real estate and many long time U.S. expatriates in Mexico
that we have interviewed over the years. Parts of
this book have been reproduced from various
U.S. State Departments' Bureau of Consular
Affairs publications.

Learn more about our lectures, guidebooks and
tours on the web at www.livingoverseas.com

Living Overseas Mexico, Copyright ©1999
Previously published as *Living and Making
Money in Mexico* ©, 1996 and 1998.

Second Edition

Printed in the United States of America 1999

ISBN: 0-9662421-3-0

Library of Congress: 97-095108

ABOUT THIS BOOK

Like all our other books, this Mexico book is lean and mean, including only information that will help the newcomer succeed in life in this Latin America hot spot.

Keep in mind prices were up-to-date as of the time of writing, but things in Mexico can change with each new *sol*.

Much has changed in Mexico since our last edition. Mexican banks now allow accounts in dollars; health insurance policies have been altered; laws governing foreign drivers have been modified; and money-making opportunities are now more varied. We'll also tell you how the Internet has changed life abroad.

We've added illustrations to this new edition. We found our artist, José Javier Ramírez, on a street corner in San Miguel de Allende where he was selling his sketches.

All prices in the book are in dollars unless stated in pesos. When calling Mexico from the U.S. or Canada first dial 011 (international direct), then 52 (country code), then the city code, and then the phone number. You'll find the city codes on our Mexico profile page.

When you see our 👍 **TIPS** icon be sure you're paying attention — that's our new symbol for insider's tips and secrets.

We haven't left out any of the valuable information that Living Overseas Books have come to represent. By skimming our pages, you'll discover where to live, how to acquire residency and open bank accounts, what type of small business is best for you, anecdotal accounts of successful expats, essential contacts for business permits and visas, how to take fullest advantage of computers and technology in your overseas venture, and much more.

We hope you enjoy this new, updated edition of *Living Overseas Mexico*. We're working hard to make it the single most informative source you can own on living, working and *succeeding* abroad. *¡Adelante!*

A FEW OF OUR
ILLUSTRATIONS
BY JOSÉ JAVIER RAMÍREZ
COMONFORT, GTO. MEXICO

Sean Godfrey
Publisher
Page 169

Mago
Facilitator
Page 197

Katie Reeder
Exporter
Page 167

Rod Collins
Internet Service
Page 168

CONTENTS

ORIGINAL ILLUSTRATIONS BY JOSE JAVIER RAMIREZ
Colibrí Bookstore, 51 • Pizzería, 78 • Alex Grattan, 80 • Dana
González, 81 • Mysterious Wall, 100 • Kiosk, 129 • Laundrymat,
148 • Dave Merryman, 166 • Katie Reeder, 167 • Rod Collins, 168
• Sean Godfrey, 169 • Spencer Shulman, 170 • Tom Thompson,
171 • Vickie Schlisizzi, 172 • Luis Rodríguez, 193 • Mago, 197
• VW Bug, 212 • Meet the Publisher, 252

MEXICO PROFILE

Official Name: United States of Mexico

Capital City: Mexico City (Distrito Federal)

Population: 93 million

Ruling Party: Partido Revolucionario Institucional (PRI)

Head of State: President Ernesto Zedillo Ponce de León

Living Environment
Pros: Very low cost of living, pro-U.S., good climate, easily obtainable residency visa, proximity to U.S. and Canada.

Cons: Diarrhea, procrastination, increasing crime

Business Environment
Pros: Stable government, NAFTA, low-cost trainable work force, great opportunities

Cons: Unstable economy, corruption and bureaucracy

Local Currency: Peso

Interest Rates: 20% on 28-day certificates

Exchange Rate: U.S. $1.00 = $9.76 pesos (peso symbol= $)

Unemployment Rate: 22% (Unofficial)

Inflation Rate: 17%

Adult Literacy Rate: 87%

Top Income Generator: Manufacturing, crude oil, tourism

GDP: $400 billion

North American Pop.: More than 500,000

Official Language: Spanish

Phone Codes: Country code = 52. It must be dialed prior to the city code and then the local number. Common city codes include Acapulco, 748; Guadalajara, 36; León, 471; Mexico City, 5; Cancún, 98; Monterrey, 83; Tijuana, 66; Toluca, 721; Veracruz, 29.

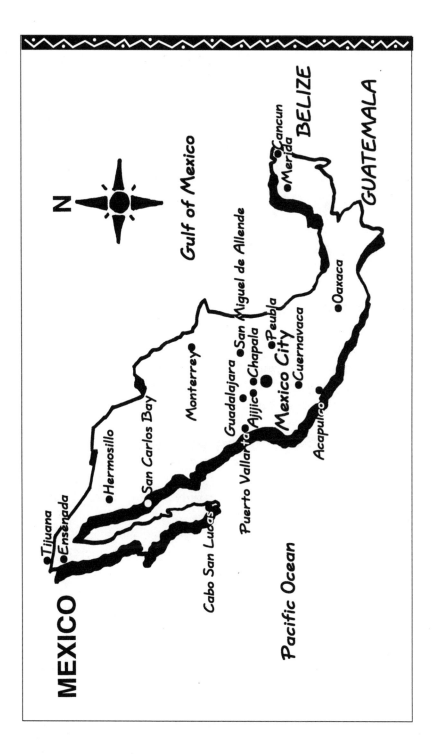

INTRODUCTION

WHO'S GOING

As recently as a decade ago, Mexico's 500,000 North American foreign population was made up mostly of retirees stretching their social security checks, employees of multinational corporations, or the bohemian crowd of artists and eccentric actors. The ones without the big bank accounts or monthly pension checks were out of luck.

In the past, Mexico fiercely limited the number of foreigners who could work and operate a business in its national territory to ensure job availability for its own citizens. The government also restricted the foreign population to only those who could support themselves with a guaranteed income from abroad.

However, these laws have been reformed and much is changing as the world's economies become global. Foreigners can live and seek employment in Mexico much easier. In addition, many of the activities once off limits to the foreign participant, including 100 percent foreign ownership of a small business, are now opening up.

This creates opportunities as never before for those *without* a guaranteed source of income, as well as the owner of a small sandwich shop or neighborhood video store, to *break the routine* and live south of the border in towns and cities which were previously inaccessible.

We've seen them come and go during our years abroad — the career business executives, disenchanted with the corporate rat-race or displaced by company down-sizing, who are ready for the chance to strike out on their own in relatively uncharted territory. Mexico represents untapped markets and the chance to put hard-owned business expertise to good use for your own good, and not someone else's.

And then there are the two-income families worried about how they're going to put their kids through school when their combined U.S. savings can barely cover a short family vacation once a year. Mexico can provide them with some much-needed additional income and the chance to bring their kids up "globally," in one of the excellent bilingual and bicultural schools.

Did we mention the adventurous types? South-of-the-border opportunities broaden the horizons of recent college grads who desire economic independence, but would rather get it by broadening their perspectives, learning another language and by overcoming the "fish out of water" feeling to achieve personal success in a foreign culture — even the most varied "corporate ladder" can rarely offer that.

The people going to Mexico are probably just like you. They have big dreams and ambitions. Some of them may not make it, but the ones who do — the ones who are flexible enough to adapt and learn — often tell us that their move south was the best decision they ever made. It's tough, but intrinsically more fulfilling than anything they experienced back home.

GO PART TIME

The world offers many temperate exotic climates, but few are as convenient for the North American as Mexico. Retirees who "winter" at a popular city like Guadalajara or resort community like Cancún have known for years the benefits of part-time overseas life.

Budget plane fares to Mexico now make it possible for expats to travel home several times a year for long weekends or even months. Part-time business owners are finding that modern communication devices like fax machines, computers with access to the Internet, e-mail and video conferencing make it easier than ever to stay on top of things at the Mexican office without missing out on important family get-togethers or business doings Stateside.

A part-time lifestyle may be just what you need to discover if life in Mexico is right for you. Can you learn the language? Adjust to customs that may seem completely illogical? Mix in and enjoy your new adopted culture in spite of initial feelings of alienation?

The only way to know for sure is to head down there for a few extended vacations. Go to the bank, use the post office, set up an Internet account, send and receive faxes, call long distance, try the restaurants, shop in the farmers' markets and grocery stores, talk to the people and to members of the foreign community. Experience what it's like to live there as a permanent resident, rather than just breeze through tourist-style, wining and dining as you go.

GETTING STARTED

Moving to another country enables you to start a new life, with new friends and experiences you won't find just moving to a different U.S. address. But that sense of adventure brings with it responsibility of knowing what you're getting into.

This book will help you figure that out, but many other valuable sources are also available. The World Wide Web, e-mail and chat boards are only a few of the more "techno-methods" of modern research that places reams of information only a mouse click away. But don't disregard the local library either. Countless books and magazine articles have been written about Mexico. A trusty librarian can help you sift through the deluge of print to find the information you need.

Once armed with data, the trick is to organize it and prepare a concrete *strategy* for your first "working vacation" in Mexico. Don't underestimate the importance of a strategy. It will help minimize the costly and time-consuming mistakes that we have seen expats make time and time again.

The following steps detail our favorite formula for success in Mexico. We suggest you read this section very carefully, and then re-read it after finishing the book.

STEP 1

Keep Your Job — Whatever you do, don't quit your regular job. You'll need the money to support yourself and your family while you formulate your overseas plans. Organize your personal and business affairs to give yourself more time and money to dedicate to your new goals in Mexico. You will need to spend at least 10 days in Mexico to get your research underway. A series of extended weekends are better than nothing, but remember that most agencies are only open Monday through Friday. Plan your investigative trips accordingly.

It may be necessary to borrow money or increase the credit limit on your credit cards (careful!). Open a line of credit at the local bank, get an ATM card (see banking section), and make sure your health insurance (see health section) is in order for overseas travel. You should have enough savings or other resources to support yourself in Mexico during the first year to get your life and business idea off the ground and make it profitable.

STEP 2

Research, Research, Research — Don't pull-up stakes and head for Mexico based on a dream or an article you read in a recent travel magazine. Do your homework first!

Take full advantage of the Internet — there is no other way to acquire up-to-the-minute information from diverse, international sources (see our Internet section). Read on-line country reports and search for English-language newspapers, books and other Mexican publications. Hundreds of web sites offer everything from real estate sales and residency to the latest exchange rate, State Department travel warnings and even how to dance Salsa.

Visit the local library and read all the magazines and trade journals you can get your hands on (see resource section). All this will help you narrow the field of potential Mexican living areas and investments. E-mail and even Internet Phone will enable you to economically "speak" to the experts — chambers of commerce, expat groups, local clubs and a host of others who are living in-country and know all too well the challenges of life in Mexico (see the Business section). If you don't have a computer, your local library probably does, but now is a good time to start thinking about licking that computer phobia, making the investment and getting on-line.

Remember, the length of time spent traveling isn't nearly as important as the preparations, contacts and appointments you make *before you leave home*. This is especially important in a big country like Mexico, where customs, dialects and climate change within a few hours' drive. Use the following checklist to help structure your research before you head south:

Yes, I ☑ this:

- ☐ Tourist arrivals and city population
- ☐ Potable water in the city
- ☐ Tropical diseases, such as dengue, malaria and cholera
- ☐ Crime
- ☐ Climate
- ☐ Proximity to an international airport
- ☐ History, music, sports
- ☐ Proximity to tourist areas or suppliers
- ☐ Business habits or customs
- ☐ Availability of trained, educated labor
- ☐ Investment incentives
- ☐ Access to the Internet
- ☐ Access to telephone lines
- ☐ Business contacts
- ☐ Personal and social contacts

STEP 3

Low-Budget Overseas Travel Book — Once you've decided on a location and a business that may possibly interest you, buy the best travel guide you can find on the country. We like Lonely Planet guides.

Use the book to plan a low-budget vacation to your city of interest, taking advantage of clean, low-priced lodging and meals.

Visit as much of the country as you can, and plan to combine a little pleasure with business. While there, use taxis and the public bus system to get around. It's confusing at first, but it's a great way to get the lay of the land and a feel for the people and culture.

STEP 4

Go, Enjoy and Network — Happy trails! Once you arrive at your area of choice, kick back and relax for a few days. Walk the city streets, cautiously sample the food and drink, get to know the people, get a feel for local customs.

Head for a clean, safe hotel ($15-$20 per night in Mexico), or try staying with a Mexican family. They will show you around town, introduce you to their friends and help you with Spanish. Check out the "roommate wanted" section of the local newspaper classifieds. You should be able to find a room in a family home for around $100 to $300 per month, including meals and sometimes laundry.

Don't rule out the local language schools. Most have a homestay program that places you with a Mexican family as you learn Spanish at the school. You can take advantage of your time outside of class to work on your overseas plans. See our listing of local language schools for more details.

Once you've settled in, get to work. Gather as much information as you can from local businessmen and women about opportunities and market challenges (see The People Who've Done It). Stop by the local office of the American Chamber of Commerce (AmCham). They can provide a wealth of information about economic conditions, investment climate, incentives, and all-important business contacts. Seek out expatriate organizations for information on living conditions and residency requirements.

If you remain undecided about which opportunity is best for you, re-read our Business Ideas chapter. Network with as many active, English-speaking business owners as you can. Find out when the American Legion, Rotary Club, Newcomers Club or Republicans or Democrats Abroad hold their meetings and attend a couple of them if you can.

Keep important names on file with their corresponding addresses, telephones, faxes, e-mails. These sources can help you clear up doubts even after you return home. The following check list may steer you in the right direction:

Yes, I ✔ this:

- ☐ English speaking, U.S. or Canadian-trained doctors
- ☐ Nearby emergency clinics or hospitals and costs
- ☐ Cost to rent or buy a home
- ☐ Bus and taxi fares and availability
- ☐ Demographics
- ☐ Business opportunities
- ☐ Bilingual schools
- ☐ Cost and availability of fresh fruits and vegetables
- ☐ Costs to dine at a fine restaurant
- ☐ First-run Hollywood movies in English
- ☐ Plays, theater, symphony, concerts
- ☐ Cable TV
- ☐ Proximity to shopping
- ☐ Is the food safe to eat in restaurants
- ☐ Do you like the local people
- ☐ Condition of roads and highways
- ☐ Where can you send/receive faxes
- ☐ Where can you access the Internet

STEP 5

Repeat Steps 2 and 4 — Chances are, you may not fall in love with the first place you visit, or, even if you do, you'll still need to do a lot of follow-up research once you head home. Narrow your focus, if necessary, and formulate more specific questions for your new overseas contacts. The next time you visit, your mission will be more specific. Try to attend club meetings this time around, and pre-schedule in-country business meetings before you leave home. Check with the airlines to get the best fare possible for your return trip. Plan to make at least two or three of these extended business trips to Mexico before you sell the house and wave good-bye to the neighbors.

If the community you visited left you with a less than spectacular first impression, hit the books — and Internet — again to help re-direct your search.

STEP 6

Learn the Language — Once your research and investigative trips result in you successfully choosing a destination and business opportunity, make an extra effort to learn Spanish.

Take a night class and do your homework. If you can speak the native language, you will be more in control of your business and less susceptible to potential scamsters.

We have seen many an overseas "virgin" fall prey to some smooth-talking, unscrupulous scam artist. Protect yourself by learning the language and culture of your new adopted country, and return as many times as it takes before you make the final move. Once you've found your niche, get busy! Remember the Living Overseas motto: Start small and build your business into a national or international contender.

RECOMMENDED READING

O ur *Living Overseas Mexico* guidebook is your best source for an easy transition to life in Mexico, but it shouldn't be the last. Many excellent publications may serve as supplements to our book. It's well worth every penny to invest in as many of these resource guides as possible. See our reference section for more recommended reading and web sites that could help you.

Doing Business in Mexico Engholm and Grimes. Prentice Hall, 1997. The best business book on Mexico, written for the micro-entrepreneur. It includes profiles of successful expats and is well worth the read.

Travelers Guide to Mexico This thick, colorful book is sold exclusively in Mexico and is the world's largest selling tourist guidebook to Mexico. We think it's the best there is. It's updated every year and features cities that are most visited by the international and domestic tourist. It also contains information on retiring, business and investments. You can order through the Internet at www.travel-mex.com or www.wotw.com/tgm or by mail Box 6-1007, Mexico, D.F. 06600 Mexico

The People's Guide to Mexico Carl Franz. John Muir Publications, 1997. This is a must read. A fun book on living, traveling, the people and little-known cultural idiosyncrasies you won't find in other books. Carl writes with immense wit, warmth and wisdom born of more than 20 years in Mexico.

Mexico Business World Trade Press, 1997. This book is called the "portable encyclopedia for doing business with Mexico." A good book to add to your library.

Lonely Planet Mexico Lonely Planet books. Every newcomer traveling to Mexico should have a copy of this book. You'll need this book to find clean, inexpensive hotels and restaurants. Buy it and use it.

Guadalajara Colony Reporter A weekly newspaper covering Guadalajara regional and national news. This is also a must for those who want to keep updated on everything affecting foreigners. Contact 9051-C Simpre Viva Rd, suite 5-452, San Diego, CA 92173 or www.guadalajarareporter.com.

Choose Mexico Howells and Merwin. Gateway Books. A good book for the retiree.

Mexico Living and Travel Newsletter A quarterly newsletter that has a good overview of foreign life in the most popular retirement area in Mexico: Guadalajara. 6301 S. Squaw Valley Rd, Suite 23, Pahrump, NV. 89048-7949

Travelers' Medical Alert to Mexico William W. Forgey, M.D. ICS Books, INC. This 132-page book is filled with preventative measures and treatments of common health problems in Mexico, such as travelers' diarrhea — good for newcomers to know before they make the move.

ABOUT MEXICO

COUNTRY

Mexico, the world's thirteenth largest nation and eleventh largest economy, is a mountainous country of breathtaking contrasts. Two-thirds of its 764,000 square miles of national territory consists of highlands between 3,200 and 8,200 feet.

Some of the higher peaks, including Pico de Orizaba at 18,400 feet and Iztaccíhuatl at 17,666 feet, are snow-covered year-round, while the country's hot, sub-tropical coastal lowlands are the site of some of the world's premier beach resorts.

The country can be roughly divided into three climate zones. The lowland hot regions with elevations up to 2,600 feet have temperatures above 80°F. (26°C.) practically year-round. Some of these regions include Tabasco, Yucatán, Chiapas and Quintana Roo.

The "temperate zone" is located between 3,000 and 6,000 feet. Guadalajara and Chapala are both located in this zone. Above this altitude it gets a little chilly. Mexico City is in this latter category at 7,300 feet above sea level.

Mexico City, also known as the Federal District or *Distrito Federal*, is the world's largest city. More than 20 million of the country's 93 million people call this, the nation's hectic capital, home.

Culturally rich and physically beautiful but with some of the world's worst air quality, Mexico City has recently hosted a campaign to control the number of cars in circulation to clean up the atmosphere.

Nearby Guadalajara is home to the world's largest population of North American expatriates, who choose the region for its temperate climate, big-city convenience and picturesque, mountainous setting.

Mexico shares a 2,000-mile border with the U.S. to the north, Guatemala to the south, Belize and the Gulf of Mexico to the east along the Yucatán Peninsula and the Pacific Ocean to the west. It is also home to Baja California, the world's longest peninsula, with 800 miles of mountains, plains, deserts and pristine beaches.

HISTORY

From as early as 1200 to 900 B.C., Mexico was dominated by bands of industrious Olmec, Mayan and Toltec Indians who built great cities and were masters of mathematics, architecture and astronomy. Their early calendars and hieroglyphic writing, complex religion and art became the foundations of the Aztec nation, which appeared in the early fourteenth century.

When Italian explorer Christopher Columbus "discovered" the new world in 1492, the warring Aztecs already controlled vast territories in Mexico, with at least 370 nations subject to their capital city of Tenochtitlán. Powerful empire-builders, the Aztecs earned the animosity of their subordinate tribes through bloody rituals and exhorbitant tribute payments.

The Aztecs failure to win the respect and loyalty of the tribes they conquered contributed to their downfall. The arrival of Spanish conquistador Hernán Cortés in 1519 corresponded coincidentally with the supposed prophetic "return" from the east of their supreme god Quetzalcoatl.

When the Indians observed the arrival of the Spanish explorers dressed in steel and riding strange animals, they assumed that they were witnessing the return of their revered god and completely surrendered to the foreigners.

Later, after the Spanish went on to brutally enslave and hideously mistreat the Indians in a greedy quest for gold, Aztec leaders realized they'd mistaken their god for those who would become the rapists of their women, the destroyers of their culture and the spreaders of diseases that would ravage their empire.

The Aztecs received little help from the smaller tribes, which, disgruntled by Aztec customs and high duties, were eager to assist the Spaniards in their oppressor's fall.

The three centuries of Spanish colonial rule that followed were dominated by religious fervor and greed for gold and silver. The Spaniards built churches and forced the natives to convert to Catholicism. Those who refused where killed as part of the bloody inquisition. Indians adopted Spanish as their language and European dress, but elements of their indigenous culture remained, intermingled with the superimposed customs.

The conquistadors were granted land holdings in Mexico, then called "New Spain," by the Spanish government, and large haciendas maintained by Indian slave labor were formed that would later give rise to violent peasant uprisings over the control of land.

Independence came to Mexico in 1822, and for the first time in 300 years, Mexicans themselves controlled their land. General Agustín Iturbide was instrumental in drafting a peace plan that put an end to the fighting. He later declared himself emperor of Mexico, but his rule was cut short by Antonio López de Santa Ana, whose opposition forces obligated Iturbide to abdicate in 1823.

The following year, a constitution was drafted and the country's first president, Guadalupe Victoria, was sworn into office, but the political situation remained anything but stable. Over the next 22 years, power in Mexico changed hands 33 times, with 11 terms held by Santa Ana, the same general who led Mexican forces at the famous battle of the Alamo against a group of northern insurgents who wanted to declare Texas an independent nation. Battles with the U.S. would result in Mexico losing two-fifths of its national territory, or what today is most of the southwestern United States.

In 1861, Santa Ana was ousted for the last time by a young Zapotec Indian from the state of Oaxaca, Benito Juárez. To this day, Juárez, who struggled against the odds to become president, remains one of Mexico's most beloved political figures. After a lost battle with France forced him to temporarily step down as president, Juárez later went on to regain his post. He is credited for the completion of the first railroad connecting Mexico City and Veracruz, as well as establishing free and obligatory education through sixth grade.

With the twentieth century came rapid modernization at the hands of military dictator Porfirio Díaz, but his policy of industrialization at all costs created large-scale unrest in the almost totally agricultural nation that culminated in the Mexican revolution of 1910. Six years of fighting with men like Pancho Villa and Emiliano Zapata brought an end to Díaz' rule and the beginning of widespread socialization of many of the country's private institutions and land holdings.

State control strengthened in the coming years and gave rise to modest economic growth. The discovery of oil in the 1980s created political confidence to borrow heavily from international lending institutions to improve oil industry infrastructure. But when international oil prices fell unexpectedly, the country found itself dangerously close to bankruptcy, with a staggering foreign debt, high inflation rates and a rapidly devaluing currency.

Former president Miguel de la Madrid changed Mexico's economic course by signing the General Agreement on Tariffs and Trade in the mid 1980s. The agreement, signed by some 116 countries, lowered tariffs and trade barriers and gave rise to increased competition, forcing Mexican industry to modernize.

Madrid's successor, Carlos Salinas, kept the reforms moving in 1990 by opening up Mexican markets, privatizing industry and banking and breaking down barriers with the country's natural trade partners, the U.S. and Canada. From these reforms, the North American Free Trade Agreement (NAFTA) was conceived.

At the height of its rapidly expanding and strengthening economy, the country experienced a paralyzing devaluation of its currency in December 1994, just when the world was speaking of Salinas' "Mexican economic miracle."

Compounding the economic woes was a bloody uprising in the mountainous state of Chiapas in January 1994, when a masked, charismatic "Comandante Marcos" led his group of "Zapatistas" in protest of the deplorable living conditions and widespread injustices among the Mayan Indians.

The violent uprising, which claimed the lives of some 500 rebels, Mexican troops and civilians spurred the government into negotiations. A peace treaty was signed later that year that still holds today, but conditions of the Mayas have not improved and emotions have been fueled by the presence of 40,000 Mexican soldiers that now surround Chiapas.

Growing restless with government inaction, the rebels have nonetheless remained true to the treaty and have continued with peaceful forms of protest. But pressure will continue to build if the government remains unresponsive.

NAFTA is firmly in place and free trade is the trend of the future. But many Mexicans, still shaken by a radical reduction in their spending power resulting from the devaluation, have adopted a "wait and see" attitude regarding their country's economic future.

In spite of its industrial might and recent modernization, Mexico still remains in many ways a developing country. An entire generation may not be sufficient to raise the country to the level of development it longs for.

GOVERNMENT

Mexico is a federal republic consisting of 31 states and a federal district. All are free and sovereign in their internal regimes, but united into a federation in accordance with the provisions of the Political Constitution of the Mexican Republic.

The Constitution is the fundamental law upon which the overall organization of the country is based. The document was enacted on Feb. 5, 1917 and remains in effect today. The federation is divided into executive, legislative and judicial bodies.

Executive power is held by the president who is elected by direct vote for one six-year term. The president cannot be re-elected.

The state governments are headed by popularly elected governors who also serve single, six-year terms. Each has his or her own state legislature and judicial system.

Since 1988, an assembly of representatives is elected every three years in the Federal District. This assembly is empowered to issue ordinances regarding the day-to-day administration of the District. All Federal District officials hold appointive offices and, as such, may serve for more than a single term, although this is unusual. In view of the size and economic importance of the District, its annual budget is considerably larger than the state budgets.

Legal System Unlike the U.S. system of common law, Mexico's judicial system is based on the French Napoleonic Code of "civil law." In a civil law system, the application of the law is based on a codification of laws and legal principles.

Politics Upon entering the 1994 election year, the ruling Institutional Revolutionary Party (PRI) had not lost a presidential election since its establishment 64 years ago. In early 1994, then President Carlos Salinas de Gotari hand-picked Luis Donaldo Colosio, the former secretary for social development, to be the PRI's presidential candidate and Salinas' probable successor.

Colosio was assassinated March 23, 1994 while campaigning in the northern border city of Tijuana. A week later, the PRI endorsed former education secretary Ernesto Zedillo, who went on to win the 1994 elections and is the current President of Mexico. The next elections will be held in 2000.

Political Issues President Zedillo has faced a number of challenges his first year in office, ranging from the collapse of the peso in December 1994 to the continuing conflict in Chiapas.

The Chiapas incident served to underscore the depth of socioeconomic and political conflicts that still exist in post-Salinas Mexico. However, it has not changed international perceptions of the country's dramatic economic metamorphosis over the past decade. Nor has Mexico's current status as a developing industrial nation suffered. It is still very much considered a country with a future.

The Zedillo administration doubled its efforts to try to close the gap between rich and poor. The country's more open political system serves as a relief valve for people to vent their frustrations at the ballot box in local elections.

And that is exactly what they did in July 1997, when for the first time since 1929, the controling Institutional Revolutionary

Party (PRI) failed to win a majority in congress. Now, the PRI must share power, as well as cope with the election of its long-time critic, Cuauhtemoc Cardenas, as mayor of Mexico City.

The PRI clearly had it coming. If it has been credited with modernizing Mexico's economy, it has also been rife with corruption, repression and brutality -- the Salinas administration was evidence of the party at both its best, and its worst.

NAFTA National support for the full implementation of the North American Free Trade Agreement (NAFTA) between the U.S., Mexico and Canada has not been altered by the recession or the unrest in Chiapas.

The U.S. alleges that the agreement will improve economic prosperity for all three of its trading partners. NAFTA's proponents consider that economic growth fostered by the agreement will help alleviate some socioeconomic conditions that contributed to the Chiapas turmoil and other conflicts. The current government is firmly behind the agreement.

Assassinations The assassinations of PRI presidential candidate Luis Donaldo Colosio on March 23, 1994 and of PRI secretary general José Francisco Ruiz Massieu only six months later, rocked the Mexican political scene.

Despite the shock and horror of these events, the Mexican system held together well, and the opposition parties put partisan politics aside to show solidarity with the nation as a whole. In an unprecedented move, President Zedillo named Antonio Lozano of the opposition PAN party attorney general. His office is currently investigating the heinous killings.

Uncertainty The recession, the uprising in Chiapas and the two assassinations have augmented uncertainty in Mexico, but the U.S. government is confident that the country's political institutions will weather the crisis. The events were a shock to the political system, which has enjoyed more than half a century of stability, but its political resilience and flexibility has been heartening.

Mexico is bound to experience some "bumps" as it makes the transition from a closed economy to an open market and from one-party dominance to a multi-party system. A key factor in Mexico's stability is its willingness to maintain a dialogue about the country's future, as well as its politicians' ability to work together to bring about change in an orderly fashion. These are the end results of a maturing political system and the culmination of many years of struggle by the opposition to have greater access to government.

ECONOMY

Since the 1910 revolution, Mexico's economy has evolved from an almost total dependence on agriculture to the overwhelming dominance of industry.

Agriculture still occupies about 25 percent of the work force cultivating crops such as corn, wheat, rice and beans, but agriculture produces only around 8 percent of the country's gross national product.

The manufacturing industry employs roughly 18 percent of the work force and is centered mainly in Mexico City. Motor vehicles, processed foods, steel, chemicals, paper, glass and textiles have overtaken the country's traditional products of coffee, sugar, zinc, copper and silver.

The northern hub city of Monterrey, only 145 miles from the U.S. border, serves as another important industrial center. Northern border towns also contribute with many small to mid-size maquila factories.

Guadalajara is Mexico's second largest city and one of its most beautiful. Originally, it was an agricultural center but has evolved toward distribution and manufacturing. Its pleasant climate and strategic location has made it a favorite location for the corporate headquarters of many foreign firms.

Mexico is a country rich in mineral resources and enjoys the world's fifth largest deposits of petroleum. Oil and natural gas produce about 28 percent of the country's export earnings. Mining today only accounts for about 3 percent of the gross national product, but the country still remains the world's largest producer of silver.

Large-scale land distribution following the revolution carved up Mexico's massive haciendas into small plots for subsistance farming. These plots, called *ejidos* were given to rural farmers to work, but could never be sold. As part of the reforms of former

President Carlos Salinas, rural workers became the owners of their *ejidos* with full rights to sell them for profit.

Only time will tell if this reform succeeds in providing a better standard of living for all Mexicans, or simply a return to pre-revolution times of huge "haciendas" concentrated in few hands and large numbers of poverty-stricken landless peasants.

The December 1994 Peso Crash Almost everyone has a theory about why the Mexican peso crashed in December 1994. Some blamed former President Carlos Salinas for borrowing and importing too much. Others say current President Ernesto Zedillo was to blame for losing control of the economy. Still others pointed to social unrest and political violence. But regardless of why it happened, the disaster succeeded in slamming the brakes on the country's ambitious economic development. The real supposed reasons for the peso's fall are complex.

A peasant uprising in the southern state of Chiapas turned bloody in 1994. The small warring farmers demanded an opening-up of the Mexican political system, overwhelmingly dominated by the ruling Institutional Revolutionary Party (PRI) since the 1910 revolution. The violence was followed with the assassinations of PRI political candidate Luis Colosio and of PRI Secretary General José Francisco Ruiz.

The violence sent shock waves through the investment community, as companies sought to pull their money out of what they perceived as a highly unstable situation. Government fiscal policy sought to sell dollars to bolster the sagging peso in an attempt to regain investor confidence. But when dollar reserves became dangerously low, widespread fear of economic collapse caused even more investors to flee. Finally, the Mexican Central Bank allowed the peso to float against the dollar, resulting on the loss of nearly half its value.

The drastic devaluation broke many small and mid-size companies that imported foreign goods to Mexico. They watched their sales evaporate as Mexican consumers, rocked by a more than 40 percent reduction in buying power, switched to less expensive domestic goods.

Larger companies with vast reserves suffered losses, but have weathered the drop. Today, surviving companies are taking advantage of their competition's exit by lowering prices in an attempt to capture more market share.

Companies who export Mexican products were affected favorably by the devaluation, as their production costs dropped dramatically. These companies are predicted to do extremely well over the next few years.

A $20 billion aid package to Mexico approved by the administration of U.S. President Bill Clinton succeeded in calming nervous investors and provided breathing room to assess damages and propose solutions. Many say the implementation of NAFTA in January 1994 kept investors in the country who would otherwise have pulled out quickly.

As relative prices readjust and monetary policy becomes less restrictive, growth and currency stability will push GDP, as measured in dollars, back to and above 1994 levels.

Three years later, the economy has rebounded beyond the expectation of even the hardened skeptics. GDP growth between April and June 1997 was almost 9 percent -- the highest quarterly growth in 16 years. Unemployment dropped to the high teens in June, and some 430,000 new jobs were created since January.

An estimated 90 percent of international stock market professionals are again beginning to recommend that their clients fatten their portfolios with Mexican stocks, whose values have more than doubled since early 1995.

Some analysts credit Zedillo's "Economic Emergency Plan" for the turn-around. The plan calls for strict control of the money supply, decreased government expenditure, no mandated cost-of-living wage increases and large-scale privatization of infrastructure. Internationally, the plan has been met with wide financial support.

But "red flags" are everywhere. Skeptics caution that the April to June GDP explosion was due to increased consumer spending brought on by lower inflation and higher employment. Spending rose on imported goods, and did little to pump money back into the economy through purchase of national goods and investment. Congresswoman Ifigenia Martínez warned that the jobs that have been created are low-wage and part-time. Meanwhile, the population keeps growing, putting pressure on still reduced spending power.

Savings are in short supply. Given the country's notorious habit of suddenly devaluing the currency, foreign investors can only be enticed by high returns. They also favor portfolio investment, which can be quickly shifted or liquidated, to tying their money up in costly infrastructure. Even those Mexicans who do have savings, don't trust the national banks; rather, they invest abroad, maintaining Mexico's continuing need for foreign capital.

Will it happen again? That's the question many U.S. and Canadian investors are currently asking themselves. In spite of the disaster, analysts maintain that Mexico's economy remains fundamentally sound. In 1994 the country achieved a balanced budget and dramatic reduction in its federal government deficit. It's industrial base is diversified. Petroleum is still a major income producer, but no longer dominates as it did in the 1980s.

Mexico is the United States' third largest export market after Canada and Japan. In turn, two-thirds of all direct investment in Mexico comes from the U.S. In spite of the trouble, U.S. exports to Mexico have continued at a slower pace. Many investors are now poised to go back in, taking advantage of rock-bottom prices, but the risk is far from gone.

In a short period of five years, the country went from "the miracle" to "the crash," but a period of bold economic and political reform now appears to be underway.

The international financial community remains cautious about Mexico, but experts predict continued modest growth, due in part to the Mexican Central Bank's commitment to sound fiscal policy.

PEOPLE

Mexicans are as diverse as the country they live in. Whether from the country or city, of indigenous or European heritage, cosmopolitan or humble, fabulously rich or strikingly poor, Mexicans are proud of who they are and relish their traditions of family, friends, business, conversation and food.

The U.S. or Canadian citizen whose concept of the "typical Mexican" goes no farther than a gang member, a poor agricultural worker with broken English or a serape-clad drunk slumped against a cactus may become a little disconcerted when confronted with the truth — a culture teeming with sophistication at all socioeconomic levels, and a people who are articulate conversationalists, expert hagglers and skilled entrepreneurs.

Newcomers to Mexico may find that their biggest frustration is not being able to participate in hundreds of intricate and animated daily discussions due to their rudimentary Spanish!

Mexicans view work differently from other North Americans. While the family lives of many U.S. or Canadian citizens often suffer because of their professional drive to succeed in the workplace, Mexicans view work as the means to achieve more time with the family, their number one priority.

Mexican businessmen and women prefer to get to know their associates before dealing with them. During any extended business lunch, Mexicans will talk extensively of their families and will ask myriad questions to delve into the personal lives of their potential associates. Few Mexicans will "get down to business" with total strangers. The business relationship is instead carefully cultivated based on personal trust and affection.

Rampant endemic corruption in public life has taught Mexicans to only trust family and friends. Friendships and favoritism are widely used to speed-up complicated procedures, achieve hard-to-accomplish goals or acquire coveted positions. The saying "It's not what you know but whom you know," applies in Mexico as no where else.

Social life in Mexico centers around family gatherings and outings. Extended families are common, with older members taking care of the children while the younger members work to support the family. Children's day-care centers are practically non-existent in all but the biggest cities.

Family life evolves around mealtime. Breakfasts are usually light, as is the evening's light dinner of sandwiches, bread, coffee or hot chocolate. The day's major multi-course meal is consumed around 2 to 3 p.m., followed by a traditional leisure time of conversation among family. The typical "two-hour" lunch at home is practiced in all but the largest cities where many people face more than an hour's commute between home and office. Afternoon work activity commences around 4 p.m. and continues until 8 p.m. Government offices are also open late.

Gregarious and curious, Mexicans often stop by local bars and cafés after work to catch up on conversation with their friends before heading home. Conversation and food occupy major roles in Mexican life. Each city's downtown district fills nightly with window shoppers, curious on-lookers and business people returning home. In small country towns, life is quieter but still revolves around the late afternoon meal and conversation.

Customs and traditions change throughout Mexico, but warmth, curiosity and generosity remain constant. Most newcomers are at first overwhelmed by the pace and energy of Mexican life, but then come to realize that much can be learned from this vital culture that has in so many ways influenced life throughout all of North America.

CLIMATE

Huge and diverse, Mexico is home to hot, sub-tropical coastal regions and snow-capped mountains.

Mexico City, Guadalajara and other cities of the Central Plateau enjoy a year-round temperate climate. At altitudes above 5,000 feet, the region never becomes really hot, even in midsummer. In an average year, Mexico City would probably register a maximum temperature of 88°F (31°C), while Guadalajara would raise the mercury to 95°F (35°C). April and May are the hottest months.

Mexico City receives little rain compared to many parts of the country, but during the June through September rainy season, showers will fall everyday, but only for a couple of hours in the afternoon. Nights and evenings can be chilly to cold. December through February are generally the coolest months throughout the country.

Temperatures are higher farther south, but rainfall varies considerably. Higher cities, such as Oaxaca (5,000 feet), are chilly to cold at night, but summer daytime temperatures could be as high as 100°F (38°C). Anywhere on the Yucatán Peninsula, daytime temperatures will be in the low eighties (upper twenties C), with nighttime temperatures seldom falling below 60°F (16°C).

Acapulco is one of the wettest coastal resorts, and receives more than 663 inches (1,700 mm) of rain per year, concentrated in the country's June to September rainy season. Other popular resorts such as Mazatlán and Cozumel, are slightly drier with showers falling intermittently all year long. Rainfall is especially high on the eastern slopes of the Sierra Madre and on the north side of the Isthmus of Tehuantepec.

The northwest region, including Baja California and the inland zone, is Mexico's driest. For additional information about specific climates, please see the Real Estate section.

THE LIVING OVERSEAS SERIES
GLOBAL LIVING AND BUSINESS INDEX

Rating a country on its livability or opportunities is based on many factors. In some countries, the benefit of a low cost of living is frequently offset by substandard health conditions or consistently inclement weather. We at LO Books have concocted a scoring system designed to give you an idea of overall conditions in Mexico.

The five categories are ranked on a scale of one to 10, with 10 being excellent. Compare how close the country's total score comes to the perfect score of 50, a mythical living and investing Utopia.

CATEGORIES

•**Cost of Living** (score 9) Mexico has one of the lowest costs of living on earth! As the peso continues to devalue against the U.S. dollar, life will become even more economical for the expatriate. Thanks to the North American Free Trade Agreement (NAFTA), most imported consumer items are now priced very competitively with national products.

Factors considered: Extremely low import duties and low cost groceries, autos, clothing, housing, health care, utilities and entertainment.

•**Health** (score 7) The Mexican Institute of Social Insurance provides the expatriate with good, low-cost health care for life, but most tap water is undrinkable, and "Montezuma's Revenge" is probable if you continue to experiment with side-street cafés and sidewalk food stands. There are many good, private hospitals.

Factors considered: Number of physicians per capita, life expectancy, diseases, low-cost medical and dental services, quality of tap water, Montezuma's revenge.

•**Living Environment** (score 9) Mexico rates high in this important category due to its varied climate zones and terrains, many coastal resorts and colonial towns. All the world's best Latin entertainment passes through or originates in Mexico, offering residents a potpourri of musical and cultural options. The Mexican government and people are pro-U.S. Mexico is so close to the rest of North America, that most residents can return home regularly without major economic hardship. Although the crime rate is growing, many expatriates continue to feel safer here than in most large U.S. cities.

Factors considered: Recently released movies available, abundance of traveling concerts and plays, relative safety, large expatriate population, many living environments, close to the U.S. and Canada.

•**Stability** (score 6) Mexico has been a friendly neighbor to the U.S. for more than 100 years, but the collapse of the peso, the revolt in Chiapas, the increasing restlessness of the Mexican worker, the 1994 political assassinations and the amount of political corruption detract from the country's stability.

Factors considered: Democratically elected government, freedom of religion, freedom of expression, social guarantees, civil liberties, internal strife and corruption.

•**Business** (score 8) The Foreign Investment Law of 1993 and NAFTA have opened the country to U.S. and Canadian investment. Political safeguards are already in place to protect the foreigner's investment, regardless of the party in office. A large, low-cost pool of easily trainable workers, proximity to the U.S. and Canada and the devaluing peso all combine to make Mexico one of the world's hottest investment regions.

Factors considered: Easily obtainable business visa for North Americans, ample opportunities and investment incentives, protection for foreigners in business and real estate ownership, labor cost and consumer capabilities.

MEXICO

Cost of Living	Health	Living Environment	Stability	Business	Total Score	Utopia
9	7	9	6	8	39	50

TEN QUICK TIPS
FOR THE NEWCOMER

The decision to move to a foreign country brings with it uncertainty, stress and even fear about adjusting to the new culture and customs. The following is a list of 10 answers to the questions most frequently asked by newcomers to Mexico:

1. Because the peso is not a stable currency, the best way to protect your money is to leave it at home. Wise foreigners open a checking account in a U.S. bank with Mexican connections or open an account with a reputable Mexican investment firm that will cash personal checks from a U.S. or Canadian bank without charge. Most foreign residents only change two to three months' living expenses into pesos.

2. Most foreigners live in Mexico on a six-month tourist visa. If you want to work, import furniture or just feel more stable in your new country, a FM-3 residency visa is becoming increasingly easier to obtain, especially as the devaluing peso puts minimum required investments within reach.

3. Foreigners relocate to certain regions of Mexico based on their needs. Working expatriates usually settle in Mexico City, Guadalajara, Monterrey or another of the business capitals. Those with tourism projects usually choose coastal areas, such as Cancún, Puerto Vallarta or Cabo San Lucas. Retirees usually relocate to popular gringo retirement communities in Lake Chapala, San Miguel de Allende or even Guadalajara.

4. Payoffs are common in all Latin countries. Don't be surprised if someone expects a little extra to get things done faster. A traffic cop may, for example, let you off the hook for 20 pesos. Once you're in Mexico for a while, you'll learn that these payoffs and other loopholes may help you get around much of the rules and regulations. A few good contacts and a little creativity will help you accomplish a lot here, but beware — laws do exist. Loopholes and payoffs should be used as the exception, never the rule.

5. Direct foreign ownership of real estate is permitted in Mexico except properties located within 62 miles from any border, or 31 miles from any coastline. However, foreigners may acquire ownership to these restricted zone properties through an easily obtainable real estate trust. No financing is available in Mexico at economically feasible rates, but a few U.S. mortgage companies are now beginning to lend on Mexican real estate.

6. Outside the country's up-scale expatriate districts, Mexico has one of the lowest costs of living in the world. In pleasant residential Mexican neighborhoods a nice home or apartment rents for around $300 per month. A monthly budget for two people including maid and entertainment shouldn't exceed $1,000 per month.

7. Socially, Mexico's expatriate communities offer everything from American Legion, bridge and garden clubs, tennis courts, golf courses, theater and ample night life. Spanish speakers will discover a fascinating, intricate mix of modern indigenous cultures that rival any other country in the world.

8. Learn Spanish. The happiest expatriates are those who fully immerse themselves in their new, adopted culture, including the language. Enroll in a good Spanish school before you re-locate. Those who arrive with a good base of vocabulary and basic understanding of grammar will speak fluently in two years or so — providing you speak Spanish regularly. Without formal instruction, learning the language could take many years. Many newcomers hire a bilingual assistant for around $200 per month to help them through the initial rough spots. This arrangement should be temporary.

9. Most expatriates feel safer in Mexico than they did in their own neighborhoods back home. The key is common sense! Take usual precautions when walking through the city, exiting the bank or carrying photographic equipment or electronics. It's a good idea to be wary, but not overly concerned about your personal safety.

10. Foreigners may start and own businesses in Mexico as long as they obtain the proper visa or business entity. Visas and business entities have become much easier to acquire thanks to the North American Free Trade Agreement (NAFTA) and Mexico's Foreign Investment Law. Most investors find that start-up costs in Mexico are far lower than back home. Foreigners wishing to work for wages in Mexico must demonstrate to the government that they possess skills not readily found among Mexican nationals.

GENERAL INFORMATION

COST OF LIVING

Mexico isn't the bargain basement travel, living and investment destination it was following the 1995 peso crash, but it continues to offer an *extremely low* cost of living by U.S., industrialized standards.

Living expenses from housing, food, cars, entertainment, health insurance, domestic help etc. are very reasonably priced, yet their quality challenges any of their U.S. equivalents.

Expatriates with dollars to spend will have an enormous economic edge as devaluation continues to eat away at the peso.

How much? Living expenses depend entirely upon your lifestyle, but no matter how you choose to live, your income will buy more in Mexico. Two people can live comfortably for less than $1,000 per month. A monthly income of $2,000 or more can provide luxuries only dreamed of in the U.S.

Real Estate There has never been a better time to buy real estate in Mexico. A new foreign investment law makes it easier for foreigners to own real estate, and prices have fallen due to the peso's devaluation. However, in many of the areas most popular with gringos, real estate prices are unaffected by devaluation because properties are usually bought and sold in dollars.

Homes in popular North American retirement areas, such as Lake Chapala, Guadalajara and San Miguel de Allende, a three-bedroom home will rent for $400 to $500 and sell for $60,000 to

$500,000. But if you look in the outskirts of the same areas, houses are selling for half those prices. In a nice "local" neighborhood of Guadalajara, for example, you can rent a three-bedroom house for $250 per month or purchase one for $30,000.

Groceries Supermarkets offer some of the same brand-name items that are sold in U.S. establishments. Imported brands cost slightly more in Mexico than they do in the U.S., but local brands for the same products can be had for considerably less. Fruits and vegetables are a real bargain in Mexico, and many expatriates prefer to buy them fresher and even less expensive at the local outdoor markets.

Many Mexicans who live in border towns cross over to the U.S. to buy canned goods and brand-name merchandise, while many of those living on the U.S. side cross over to Mexico to save money on fresh fruits and vegetables.

Restaurants serving fine cuisine from all over the world abound in Mexico, and low prices allow dining out three times a week or more. At the four-star Intercontinental in Guadalajara a complete meal won't cost more than $7.00 to $8.00. First-run

AVERAGE MONTHLY BUDGET FOR TWO PEOPLE

Rent....................................	$300.00
Housekeeper...........................	70.00
(Five days/week, part time)	
Food....................................	200.00
Electricity/Gas......................	30.00
Water...................................	10.00
Telephone (local calls)...............	15.00
Transportation (bus - taxi)..........	30.00
Entertainment (once a week)........	80.00
Health Insurance....................	50.00
Miscellaneous.......................	100.00
Total:	**$885.00**

movies in English from the U.S. cost only $2.00 per person.

With servants' salaries so low, you can hardly afford not to hire a full or part-time maid, cook or gardener. A full-time, live-in help costs from $100 to $300 per month, and you'll pay only around $5.00 per day for part-time services.

Utilities are also reasonable. Electricity runs around $15.00 for a two-bedroom house. Telephone service costs $15.00 per month for basic service. Propane gas runs $13.00 per month, and potable water service will cost another $10.00.

COST OF COMMON CONSUMER ITEMS

Tuna (One can, local brand)	$0.60
Kellogg's Corn Flakes, 540 g.	$2.50
Bacon, 1 lb.	$3.52
Bananas, 1 lb.	$0.19
Tomatoes, 1 lb.	$0.46
Toilet paper, pack of four rolls	$0.91
Sirloin steak, 1 lb.	$1.90
Soft drinks per 2-liter bottle	$0.89
Milk, 1 liter	$0.60
Domestic beer per bottle	$0.40
Bottled water, 1 gallon	$1.04
Whole chicken	$0.85
Eggs, 1 dozen	$1.11
Bacardi rum, 946 ml.	$5.00
Cuervo Special tequila, 1 liter	$5.50
Ground beef	$1.61 lb.
T-bone steak	$3.02 lb.

Cars in Mexico are priced slightly higher than in the U.S., so many North Americans choose to use their own vehicle during their time here, but driving a car with Mexican license plates offers several advantages (see *Cars in Mexico* section). The best value in town is the new, made-in-Mexico Volkswagen Beetle which sells for a modest $6,000. A fine used car can be purchased for $3,000. Premium gasoline costs $1.54 per gallon.

Health care in Mexico is adequate and inexpensive. The Mexican National Health Insurance (IMSS) will cover all an expatriate's health needs for around $290 per year. Most foreign residents choose to have complicated procedures done in the U.S. Dentists charge around $25.00 for a general cleaning and $25.00 to fill a cavity.

How far does the dollar go in Mexico? As a rule of thumb, you would have to spend at least twice the income each month to maintain an identical lifestyle farther north, without sacrificing quality of life. For $1,000 per month, a couple can live comfortably, and for $2,000, live in luxury.

TIPS *The key to low-cost living in Mexico is to adopt many of the same habits as the locals. Don't go to expensive grocery stores that feature products imported from the States. Go instead to the local outdoor food markets.*

Don't rent or buy a home in expensive gringo enclaves -- live in a Mexican neighborhood for less.

Use the Internet to communicate with family and friends back home, and only tip for exceptional service in restaurants, taxis and other "tipable" situations -- you'd be surprised how these constant tips add up!

SALARIES

As in most developing countries, the distribution of wealth between different segments of the population is uneven. The standard of living of those in upper and middle-management positions is more or less comparable to that of people who occupy similar positions in industrialized countries. However, the earnings of office, skilled, semiskilled and unskilled workers are considerably below those of their industrialized country counterparts.

One of Mexico's biggest problems is providing gainful employment for its rapidly increasing population. Unemployment and underemployment are considerable and have increased in recent years, although no comprehensive statistical information is available. The unskilled labor pool is very large in many parts of the country, particularly outside Mexico City, where the labor force has proved to be easily trained for semiskilled and skilled jobs.

The Mexican government establishes a minimum wage scale that must be observed by employers for all types of jobs. Only inexperienced workers receive the base salary, since experience, training and demand usually lead to better wages. The following list should give you an idea about average Mexican wages paid for common jobs.

Administrative or Finance Manager	$1,000/month
General Accountant	$800
Store Clerk	$175
Computer Operator	$400
Professional	$900
Bilingual Secretary	$375
Receptionist	$200
Cashier	$170
Messenger	$165
Guard	$200
Minimum wage for day's labor	$3.40/day

BUSINESS HOURS

Business offices normally open at 8:30 a.m. or 9 a.m. for an eight-hour work day with one or two hours for lunch between 2 p.m. and 4 p.m. The two-hour lunch period is almost universal outside of Mexico City.

Banks are open from 9 a.m. to 1:30 p.m., and for limited transactions from 4 p.m. to 6 p.m. The official work day for government offices is from 8 a.m. to 2:30 p.m., but has been extended to 7 p.m. in many departments. All are on a five-day week. Factories usually open at 7 a.m. or 8 a.m.

The limited hours to conduct banking and your business errands is probably one of the biggest frustrations North Americans encounter. If you want to live happily in Mexico, this is something you will have to get used to.

POST OFFICE

Businesses rarely use local postal service for international correspondence, favoring the faster and more secure private courier services of companies such as Federal Express, D.H.L., United Parcel Service or the Mexican postal service.

Mexico has many private mail services with mail-forwarding offices based in Texas or California. These services are faster and much more secure than domestic mail and cost around $10.00 per month.

The national postal service has greatly improved it's domestic service over the last two years.

The national post office (Oficina de Correos) sells stamps (estampillas) and can dispatch letters and packages by land or air. Mail can be certified (certificado).

Mexicans consider it bad manners to lick stamps, which are well-handled by postal workers. They always provide a moistened sponge for convenience.

Post office boxes are available for a small yearly fee, but be prepared for a long waiting list at most branches.

Service is slow by U.S. standards. Packages are frequently "lost" in the system. Private mail companies are at least twice as fast.

TIPS *Do yourself a favor. Ask around to find a reliable PRIVATE postal company to handle your incoming and outgoing mail. These private mail forwarding companies, like Mail Boxes Etc., give you access to most services provided by the U.S. Postal Service and private couriers. Their systems are faster and safer than conventional Mexican mail.*

TELEPHONE SERVICE

Teléfonos de México (Telmex) no longer has a monopoly on the country's telecommunications. Competition between long-distance providers is heating up, with Telmex, Alestra and Aventel as the three main players.

Delays of up to three months for a new phone line are common, so it's always best to make sure your new Mexican residence already has phone service. If you expect to receive many calls, a second phone line is highly recommended.

To obtain a phone in Mexico without posting a bond, you must have an FM-2 or FM-3 resident status. Phone lines cost approximately $320 for a residential line and $535 for a commercial line. If you move your home or business, Telmex will transfer your phone lines to your new location for approximately $150. An experienced expat or one of your new Mexican friends should be able to help you wade through the bureaucracy at Telmex.

Telephone bills can be paid at some banks and supermarkets, or at the nearest telephone company office.

Mexico's numerous cellular phone companies offer quality, inexpensive service. Foreigners must have a residency visa to obtain a cellular phone.

Calling from a public telephone in Mexico can be frustrating. Many different models confuse the novice user. Some operate conventionally with coins, others require the new Ladatel telephone card and still others are free. Ladatel cards sell for $30, $50 and $100 pesos and can be purchased at most pharmacies, markets or corner kiosks.

In addition to public telephone booths, all towns have private *casetas de larga distancia*, which are small offices with four or five telephones to make long distance or local calls. Each caseta is attended by a clerk who dials your number and keeps track of the length of the call. You can call collect, or pay for the call with cash or credit card. Most casetas also have fax facilities.

TIPS *All expats want their own telephones at home. If phones are hard to come by in your area, and you are renting, ask your landlord to give you access to his/her line. A deposit is normally charged, but it's well worth it until you get a line of your own.*

With the opening of long-distance service, many reports have come in of fraud and piracy. Be sure to check your phone bill for "phantom calls."

An English-language bookstore is a must in cities and towns popular with foreign residents. It often serves as a favorite meeting and gossip place for the expat community.

CURRENCY

Currently, both new pesos and old pesos are in circulation in Mexico. All prices are quoted in pesos without distinguishing between the two, but after you've been in Mexico for a while, you'll be able to tell the difference.

As a result of the 1993 currency reform, all prices in old pesos were divided by 1,000 to arrive at their new peso equivalents. New peso bank notes and coins were then introduced to circulate along with old peso notes and coins. The sign for pesos is "$," the same as the dollar sign.

The new peso is divided into 100 centavos. Coins come in denominations of five, 10, 20 and 50 centavos, and one, two, five 10, 20 and 50 pesos. There are notes of two, five, 10, 20, 50 and 100 pesos.

Old pesos, which are no longer being minted or printed, come in denominations of 50, 100, 200, 500 and 1,000 peso coins and 2,000, 5,000, 10,000, 20,000, 50,000 and 100,000 notes.

In popular tourist areas, U.S. dollars are readily accepted in many hotels and other establishments, but the peso predominates outside these areas. Some places will accept dollars in payment but will pay such a skewed exchange rate that you'll wish you'd changed money beforehand.

LANGUAGE

Spanish is the national language of Mexico. It is spoken and understood by all but a very small number of indigenous tribes in the interior. Indian languages are also spoken by fairly large numbers of the population in certain areas. English is also understood by many members of the business community in the capital, in larger cities and in towns that border the U.S., and in all resort areas.

TIPS *Learning to speak Spanish should become your biggest priority. You don't want to be one of the many 10-year residents we know who still have a hard time asking for coffee in the language of their adopted country.*

Learn the basics by attending a good, intensive language school, for at least a month, full time. Speak Spanish as much as you can at home and in public. Expat's who are talkative by nature have a real advantage over shy ones when it comes to learning the language. No matter how ridiculous you think you sound, Mexicans will appreciate your effort.

Once you think you have the basics, never stop studying the language. Carry a pocket dictionary with you to look up new words on the spot. Study the grammar and ask good Mexican friends to correct you when you make mistakes. Keep taking classes to improve your grammar and pronunciation.

Then, practice, practice, practice -- with your maid, with the taxi driver, with any Mexican who wants to strike up a conversation. Accept invitations to visit the homes of Mexican friends to thoroughly immerse yourself in the language. If you keep this up, you should be able to hold your own in about a year.

TOURIST VISAS

A tourist card, available at all Mexican Consulates or Embassy in the U.S., through travel agents that specialize in Mexico or on the plane en route, allows visitors to travel throughout the country for six months. The card, valid for six months, is exclusively for tourist purposes; however, any foreigner who conducts business while in the country on a tourist card may be expelled.

U.S. and Canadian citizens now have access to a 30-day North American Free Trade Agreement visa or "FM-N." Designed for foreigners who need to enter Mexico on business, the visa can be as easily acquired as a tourist card by businessmen and women employed and paid by a company in their country of origin.

HOLIDAYS

North Americans are often bewildered by the long list of Mexican holidays and religious celebrations. The following list contains the holidays when the American Consulate, Mexican banks, businesses and government offices are closed:

Jan. 1	New Year's Day
Feb. 5	Mexican Constitution Anniversary
March 21	Benito Juárez' Birthday

March or April	Holy Thursday, Good Friday and Easter Sunday
May 1	Labor Day
May 5	Anniversary, Battle of Puebla
May 10	Mother's Day
Sept. 16	Independence Day
Oct. 12	Día de la Raza
Nov. 2	Día de los Muertos (All Soul's Day)
Dec. 12	Virgin of Guadalupe Day
Dec. 25	Christmas Day
Dec. 31	New Year's Eve

Holidays and religious processions are a big part of Mexican culture. Be prepared to celebrate just about anything with special masses, folk dances, fireworks displays, parades and long processions with bands and teenage kids dressed in regional costumes.

BOOKSTORES

Sanborn stores, located in all of Mexico's major cities, stock English language books and magazines, but the best selections will be found in Mexico City (*Distrito Federal*), Guadalajara and Monterrey. Most "expat" towns have small, English bookstores. Popular shops include Sandi's in Guadalajara and American Bookstore and Britanica's in both Mexico City and Guadalajara.

NEWSPAPERS AND MAGAZINES

The following publications specializing in life and business in Mexico are available in English. See appendix for ordering information.

Magazines	Newspapers
Mexico Business	The News
Mexico Finance	El Financiero
Business Mexico	Mexico City Times
	The Colony Reporter

HEALTH

Major health threats in Mexico include pulmonary infections, typhoid, paratyphoid, tetanus, intestinal disorders and the usual contagious diseases found in every large city (see health chapter). Newcomers are most commonly victims of diarrhea, hepatitis and amebic dysentery. A strict regimen of precaution and cleanliness will avoid these problems.

Adequate health care is available in all major cities. Health facilities in Mexico City and Guadalajara are excellent. Care is limited in remote areas. U.S. medical insurance is not always valid outside the U.S. In some instances, supplemental medical insurance with specific overseas coverage and medical evacuation coverage has proven useful.

Air pollution in Mexico City and Guadalajara is severe, especially from December to May. For additional health information, contact the Centers for Disease Control's international travelers hotline at (404) 332-4559, Internet http://www.cdc.gov/. Smokers are generally not segregated in Mexico the way they are in the U.S. and other countries. Most restaurants and some of the larger hotels offer non-smoking sections, so be sure to ask. The farther you travel from the large cities, however, the less segregation you'll encounter.

👍 **TIPS** *Montezuma's Revenge is not as prevalent as you probably hear. Many long-time expats report back that after years of living in Mexico, they never once got sick from food or water. Follow the safety precautions we mention in this book and, with a little luck, you'll be OK.*

UTILITIES

Electricity is expensive in Mexico, so most homes use gas appliances. It's a good idea to contact the gas company shortly before you move into your new residence, so gas will be available right away.

Water is scarce in Mexico City due to its high, 7,350-foot elevation, but the days of low, government-subsidized water prices are coming to a close.

The recent introduction of private water companies will most certainly raise the rates. Some homes pay a flat rate for water due to the absence of water meters, but as privatization continues, meters will become universal and rates will depend on consumption.

The state-owned Federal Electricity Commission (*Comisión Federal de Electricidad*) controls all energy distribution, and power outages are common, especially during the May to September rainy season. Always keep plenty of candles on hand and new batteries in the flashlight. Surge protectors should always be used with sensitive electronics such as stereos and computer equipment. Electrical current is the American standard 110 volts. Utility bills can be paid at some banks, supermarkets and the nearest utility office.

Be sure to keep all telephone and utility bills -- these companies have been known to demand proof of payment months, or even years later.

TRANSPORTATION

Latin America is noted for its excellent public transportation and Mexico is no exception. Buses run on irregular schedules due to numerous traffic jams, protest marches and other obstacles, but are plentiful and inexpensive.

Most business people get around by taxi, which are very economical. In larger urban centers such as Mexico City, Guadalajara and Monterrey, taxis sometimes serve particular zones. Using the city's familiar yellow and green cabs, it should cost you around $2.00 to cross the city. Most city fares are regulated by meters. Some, however, are regulated either by zones or negotiation.

Hotel taxis are usually unmarked, more comfortable and more expensive. Most hotels are happy to arrange day-long excursions with the same driver. *Sitio* taxis can be reserved by telephone, usually without advanced notice. Sitio fares run from $5.00 to $7.00 / hour.

Only tourists tip street taxi drivers, although it is more common to tip a *sitio* driver. Cabbies often don't have change, so be prepared before you get in.

Buses are the main mode of transportation for most Mexicans, so even the smallest towns have bus stations. Bus travel is an excellent option for long-distance travel. A first-class, one-way ticket for the six-hour trip from Guadalajara to Puerto Vallarta costs around $20.00.

First-class busses are modern, air conditioned, have bathroom facilities, show movies in English and even include lunch and a drink. Second-class buses are a little older, and seating is on a first-come, first-serve basis, with standing room only. People have been known to stand for seven to 10-hour trips!

TIPS *We LO Bookers always travel by bus when we're investigating a new country or city. It's the best way to become familiar with the country and its people.*

__Taxicab Crime__ Avoid hailing Volkswagen bugs and other taxis from the street. Assaults and robberies on passengers are becoming more frequent. U.S. Embassy employees are advised to use only taxis from authorized taxi stands (CTO or "sitio" stands), especially upon arrival in Mexico City.

GREETINGS

As in the rest of North America, people in Mexico shake hands when meeting each other for the first time. After establishing a closer relationship, an embrace with a pat on the back is common. Women may greet men or other women with a kiss on the cheek.

In a business setting, especially when first introduced, it is important to address men by the courtesy title of *señor* (sen YOR), single women as *señorita* (sen yor EE tah) and married women as *señora* (sen YOR ah), along with their last name. Example: *Señor* Martínez, *Señorita* Rodríguez.

It is common etiquette to use professional titles with business contacts. The following are the most frequently heard:

Licenciado/a — All lawyers and anyone with a college or master's degree are referred to as licenciado.

Doctor/a — All medical doctors and anyone with a Ph.D. are referred to as doctor.

Ingeniero/a — Anyone with an engineering degree is referred to as ingeniero.

Arquitecto/a — Architects are also referred to using the professional title, arquitecto.

The feminine ending (a) should be used when addressing female professionals. A male engineer is an *ingenier<u>o</u>*, while a female is an *ingenier<u>a</u>*, etc.

TIPPING

Restaurant tips run 10 to 15 percent of the total amount before the 15 percent sales tax is added. It is not necessary to leave a tip in inexpensive diners or cafés, unless you are waited on. The following list contains usual tips for services rendered:

Grocery bag boys	$0.35
Parking lot attendants	$0.20
Valet attendants	$0.70
Gas station attendants	$0.35
Delivery people	$0.70
Windshield washers	$0.20
Taxi drivers	Nothing
Restaurant staff	10 to 15 percent of bill before taxes

A value-added tax (VAT) at the general rate of 15 percent is payable on sale of goods, services and restaurants. In "free zones," 10 percent is charged.

DOMESTIC HELP

Domestic help is much more common in Mexico than in the U.S. Servants' wages are low, but trained servants are rare. They rarely speak English and most prefer not to live on the premises. Wages for a live-in maid average $100 to $300 per month, depending on the size of the residence and her responsibilities. Room and board is extra. An experienced gardener asks from $2 to $5 per hour. Most larger residences have servants' quarters.

You can also have a maid stop by once or twice a week for a few hour visit. Part-time cooks or cleaning women usually expect around $3.00 to $5.00 per visit. Ask your friends and neighbors for references.

Mexican Labor Law imposes a number of specific obligations concerning sick leave, conditions of separation etc. The Consulate has a list of local attorneys who may be consulted to clarify these obligations.

BRINGING YOUR PETS

Documents required to bring your pet into Mexico are:

1. Certificate of vaccination against rabies (dogs and cats).
2. Certificate from veterinarian that the animal is in good health.
3. International sanitary transit permit.

All of the above documents must be verified by the Mexican Consulate nearest your place of residence in your home country. For returning pets to the U.S., contact the U.S. Customs Service or order the pamphlet entitled "Pets and Wildlife." It is available through U.S. Customs or from the U.S. Government Printing Office in Washington D.C. This pamphlet provides detailed information on entry requirements for animals and birds.

CRIME

Mexico has experienced a substantial increase in political violence over the last few years. The uprising by indigenous peasants in Chiapas in January 1994, the assassination of ruling party presidential candidate Luis Donaldo Colosio and a series of kidnappings of high-profile business leaders have kept investors and financial markets on edge. Mexico's recent economic slowdown has also contributed to a substantial increase in street crime.

Crime in Mexico City has risen in recent years, especially since the 1994 devaluation of the peso, which gave rise to higher-than-usual unemployment.

However, violent crime that has become almost commonplace in most U.S. cities is generally absent from Mexico's smaller cities and towns. Most homes and businesses have bars on their windows as a precaution against common burglars.

Choose your residence carefully. It should be in a good neighborhood with well-lighted streets. Make sure your home's entry way is also lighted and that it has a sturdy outer gate. In many neighborhoods, residents pay a security guard to patrol the streets 24-hours a day. It's also a good idea to pay someone to look in on your home daily when you're out of town. Information on specific neighborhoods may be available through the U.S. Consulate in Mexico.

Street Crime Most frequently reported crimes involve robberies and assaults of taxi passengers. Armed robbery, pickpocketing and purse-snatching are also common. In some cases, tourists have reported that uniformed police officers are the perpetrators of these crimes, stopping vehicles and then seeking money or assaulting or robbing tourists late at night.

Teller Machine Crimes Foreigners should be very cautious using all-night teller machines (ATM's) and cards. Users are frequent targets by thugs, who sometimes beat their victims to discover their access codes. In a few cases, victims have been forcibly held overnight to use the card again the following day.

Do your ATM banking in broad daylight, and choose machines that are highly visible, located in large, protected facilities, such as shopping centers or glass-enclosed security booths.

ATM and credit card holders need also be careful when ordering beverages at local night spots. Some establishments have been known to poison or drug their drinks to gain control over the patron. Victims, who are almost always unaccompanied, have been robbed of personal property and forcibly held while their ATM or credit cards were used around the city.

Metro Robberies Theft aboard the Metro, Mexico's commuter train, are becoming more frequent in Mexico City. Hold your valuables tightly and avoid using the train during busy commuting hours.

Bus Robberies Reports are increasing of thugs who board long-distance buses as passengers and then rob the real passengers when the trip is underway. It is best and safest to comply with the thieves' demands.

Kidnapping Kidnappings of both foreigners and Mexicans is increasing. U.S. businesses with offices in Mexico or concerned U.S. citizens may contact the U.S. Embassy in Mexico to discuss precautions.

Highway Crime Bandits frequent dark, rural roadways, especially at night. Criminals, particularly in Sinaloa, sometimes represent themselves as Mexican police or other local officials. Highway 15 and Express Highway 1 (limited access) in Sinaloa have been particularly dangerous. Assaults and murders have occurred along these routes both during the day and at night.

Highway hold-ups in the State of Campeche have become bolder. Long-distance buses traveling at night are the bandit's favorite targets, although day assaults have also been reported.

The U.S. Embassy strongly advises against any nighttime travel, especially by bus in the State of Campeche. The route to and from the city of Escarcega in Campeche is especially troublesome, but no night bus route can be considered safe. It's best to steer clear of these areas.

All crimes should be reported to the local authorities or to your corresponding embassy.

Drugs Penalties for drug offenders are severe. Sentences for possession of drugs in Mexico can be as long as 25 years, plus fines. Purchase of controlled medication requires a doctor's prescription.

The Mexican list of controlled medication differs from the U.S. list, and Mexican public health laws concerning controlled medication are unclear. The U.S. Embassy recommends that foreigners exercise caution when purchasing pharmaceuticals in Mexico. U.S. citizens possessing doctor-prescribed medicines have been arrested and the drug confiscated, especially in the State of Nuevo Laredo.

Possession of excessive amounts of psychotropic drugs, such as Valium, may result in arrest if the authorities suspect abuse.

More than one-third of all illicit drugs pass through Mexico on their way north. We advise foreigners to stay away from all illegal drugs. Police can arrest you and throw you in jail for an unlimited time if they even suspect you are involved.

Whew! Who would ever want to live in such a crime-infested den of darkness as Mexico? We can't write a book about Mexico without touching on crime, but don't let this discourage you. Many expat's feel safer in Mexico than they do back home. Most potentially dangerous situations can be avoided by using simple common sense.

MARRIAGE

The U.S. generally accepts as legal the marriage certificate of two U.S. citizens who were married in Mexico, but its always best to check the laws of your particular state before you say "I do" south of the border.

Foreigners who wish to marry a Mexican national in Mexico face a more complicated landscape. Church and state were totally separated here in the 1860s so, even if you're Catholic, a church wedding isn't legal without a corresponding civil marriage by a justice of the peace (*juez civil*).

The civil service usually takes place months before the church service, and some very young Mexican women may not agree to live with her husband until both services take place. Foreigners also need special permission from the Department of the Interior (*Secretaría de Gobernación*) in order to marry a national.

During the civil ceremony, a couple must stipulate what will happen to their goods should they later divorce. Each may choose to retain their individual ownership of the goods they bring into the marriage (*bienes separados*). In this case all debts and assets registered to each spouse will remain his or hers after the divorce. If the couple decides to unite their assets (*sociedad legal*), their individual names will remain on each of their goods, but in the case of divorce equal responsibility and possession will be assumed by each.

To avoid the complications and bureaucracy, many couples choose to get married in the U.S.

BIRTHS

Any baby born in Mexico is legally a Mexican citizen regardless of the parents' nationality. A child may maintain dual citizenship until the age of 18, after which he or she is expected to decide between the two. It is sometimes possible to maintain both nationalities beyond the 18-year limit if the individual can prove living or working ties in both countries.

DIVORCE

If both parties are in agreement, a divorce in Mexico is relatively inexpensive and quick. The divorce lawyer will probably charge based on the divorcing couple's combined assets, and the entire process should take from six to eight weeks.

U.S. citizens often travel to Mexico for a quick, cheap divorce by a Mexican civil judge. The U.S. generally accepts a certified translation of the divorce, but it's highly recommended to review the laws of your home state. Mexican judges try to divide the foreign couple's assets based on the laws of their state.

The Mexican divorce contract provides for custody of the children, division of property and alimony payments, among other conditions. While the Catholic church doesn't recognize divorce, today Catholic Mexican women often remarry.

RELIGION

Ninety five percent of the Mexican population is Roman Catholic. Mexicans are a deeply religious people, and the Catholic church remains powerful. Attempts at family planning continue to meet serious resistance by the church. Also, the government has had to tolerate many technically illegal religious holidays due to church influence.

Catholicism influences the lives of even the most dedicated agnostic. Throughout Mexico, church bells are sure to awaken light sleepers. Many everyday expressions have religious undertones.

Other religions, including Judaism, Protestantism and Evangelical Christianity are tolerated.

The common exclamation "¡Dios mío!" (My God!) may work its way into your own vocabulary out of frequency. Taxi drivers often make the sign of the cross when they pass by churches -- which, in some towns, are located on every block!

SHOPPING

All large Mexican cities have large, modern shopping malls with a good selection of fashionable clothes and the latest electronics. Many deluxe supermarkets sell not only groceries, but clothing, electronics and household goods. In spite of the country's well-stocked shelves, many upper-middle class families still plan a trip to Texas or California once or twice a year to bring back the latest innovations.

Outside the major population centers, merchandise variety and selection declines, but every town has a marketplace called *el mercado*, made up of individual stalls where vendors sell everything from fresh fruits, vegetables, spices, meats and milk to clothing and household items. Price haggling is customary here.

The mercado is also an excellent place to socialize or eat an inexpensive, hearty, fresh meal.

Mexican grocery stores have some U.S. food products, but most are national brands. In expat areas you are sure to find a supermarket that specializes in your favorite brand foods, but be prepared to pay a little extra.

When you feel the need for a little good old U.S.-style commerce, head for Price-Costco, Good Sam, K-Mart, Blockbuster Video or one of the many other U.S. franchise firms operating in Mexico.

BUREAUCRACY

A good sense of humor will help a lot in dealing with the frustrations of Mexican bureaucracy. Be prepared for long delays in business transactions that require paperwork, such as insurance claims, health care and driver's licenses. Also expect long waiting lines at the bank and at airport customs.

TIPS *Bring a good book, wear comfortable shoes and arm yourself with patience when running government-related errands. You are guaranteed to find an already forming waiting line, no matter how early you seem to show up. Banks are the worst.*

CLOTHING

Conservative clothing is recommended in a business setting. Men should always wear a suit and tie. Women should also dress in conservative business suits. The same attire is suitable for business gatherings in upscale restaurants.

Light cotton clothing is advisable, and a light jacket may be required on some chilly evenings. At coastal resorts, it is common for men to wear a short-sleeved shirt without a jacket, even in the more exclusive restaurants. Shorts are generally not worn by men or women in the business districts of major cities.

In higher altitudes, light clothing is customary during the summer for daytime wear. During the evening some may prefer a light wrap or jacket. In the winter, light wool clothing is comfortable during the day. Warm coats are advisable for early hours and night. Warmer clothing is frequently required inside offices and houses from December to February, as nights can be cold and few buildings have heating. The coastal areas are semi-tropical, and summer wear is used all year.

AUTO ACCIDENTS

Anyone involved in an auto accident should contact his or her local insurance adjustor or, if this is impossible, the nearest U.S. Consulate. The consulate will help contact the adjustor or an attorney, if necessary.

Whether at fault or not, motorists involved in accidents are almost always detained until an agreement has been reached and a bond placed to guarantee payment of damages or claims. If personal injuries are involved, the seriousness of the injury will determine the responsibility of the driver. In addition to impounding automobiles, officials may detain anyone involved in the accident — particularly if he or she does not have Mexican liability insurance — until injury and damage claims are settled.

A Mexican insurance policy is recognized by the authorities as a guarantee of payment for damages incurred. Presentation of the policy assists in bringing about early release.

All parties are usually asked to appear at a hearing the next day. When an agreement is reached on payment of any damages, the traffic fine, if any, is collected and the automobile is released. All those involved should save their release papers as evidence that the case is closed, especially if the car shows obvious damage.

HIGHWAY CONDITIONS AND SIGNS

Mexico's network of high-quality toll roads is expanding rapidly. During and after the summer rainy season, roads may contain dangerous breaks in the pavement and pot holes.

Mexico's fleet of "Green Angels" patrol twice a day all roads frequented by tourists to assist anyone stranded or in otherwise need of help. The Angels speak English and are trained in automechanics. They also carry first aid kits, tools and extra fuel. They don't charge for their service, but would gladly accept any donation you'd care to give.

Gasoline and oil are available in all principal towns. Leaded gas is sold as "Nova" and unleaded as "Magna Sin." Most gas stations sell unleaded gasoline. It's a good idea to buy gas often — it's sometimes a long way to the next station! Many small-time repair shops you'll encounter along the way can take care of minor repairs and fix tires, but spare parts are scarce outside the major cities and may be non-existent for cars not common in Mexico.

TIPS *All the usual Mexican daytime driving hazards — cows, dogs, potholes etc. are doubly dangerous at night. After sundown, it's best to avoid driving through the outskirts of cities and towns.*

FREE ZONES

Northern border towns and northern Baja California are considered "Free Zones" or *Zonas Libres* by the Mexican government. Immigration and customs regulations are eased in these zones, facilitating the tourist's entrance and exit. A tourist visa or automobile permit is not required in these zones, but the maximum stay established by law is 72 hours. Tourists who enter by car are recommended to insure the vehicle through a Mexican insurance company.

TIME

Most of Mexico operates on Greenwich Mean Time, which is equivalent to Chicago, Dallas and Winnipeg on winter time. The states of Baja California Sur, Sinaloa, Sonora and Nayarit follow U.S. Pacific Standard Time.

Northern Baja California has always observed the same time schedule as its U.S. neighbor, California, but a few years back the entire country switched to daylight savings time or "spring one hour forward" from the first Sunday in April to the end of October. Sought as an energy-saving measure, the government's 1988 attempt to switch to daylight savings time was revoked by popular demand.

HUNTING AND FISHING

Foreigners must have the proper permit to hunt or fish in Mexico. A special department called the "Organizers" was established with the authority to issue gun permits and fishing licenses for non-residents. Permit processing takes about two weeks, so it's a good idea to plan your trip ahead.

Foreigners may bring two shotguns or rifles into Mexico. The carrier's name, passport number, address and a description of the firearm including gauge or caliber and serial number must be registered with the "Organizers." A letter of authorization from your local police department must also be presented.

Fishing licenses are easier to obtain and are issued for fresh or saltwater. The licenses are issued by the Department of Fisheries (*Departamento de Pesca*) and may be obtained for one week, one month or one year.

For complete information about hunting and fishing in Mexico, contact Sanborn's in Mexico City or call their U.S. number 800-222-0158. They'll provide expert advice and assistance.

MEXICO CITY DRIVING RESTRICTIONS

To control air pollution, Mexico City authorities have a program restricting traffic circulation in the metropolitan area. The last digits of the license plate number determines which vehicles may not be driven on certain days of the week, as follows:

If the final digits are:	The vehicle may not circulate on:
5 & 6	Mondays
7 & 8	Tuesdays
3 & 4	Wednesdays
1 & 2	Thursdays
9 & 0	Fridays

This regulation applies to all vehicles, including cars with non-Mexican license plates. If you drive on the prohibited day, you will be fined and the car impounded for 24-hours.

THE PIROPO

In Mexico, men don't conceal their appreciation of feminine beauty, and call out an appreciative *piropo* as a woman walks by. These catcalls, more akin to a U.S. construction site, are completely accepted demonstrations of male virility, south of the border. Most piropos and the men or *piroperos* who make them are generally complimentary, but can sometimes be quite vulgar, depending on the part of town and the amount of alcohol consumed beforehand. Mexican women generally ignore them.

Among the high-school or college crowd, women will also jokingly say a *piropo* to a male friend walking by. This age bracket has a vocabulary all its own that usually incorporates many words in English. Here are a few of the most common piropos, used with "adiós," which, aside from meaning "good-bye," is also a form of greeting among passers-by on the street.

¡Adiós, morena!	Hey there, dark woman!
¡Adiós, rubia!	Hey there, blondie!
¡Adiós, linda!	Hey, pretty woman!
¡Adiós, mamacita!	Hey, little mamma!
¡Adiós, chula!	Hey there, cutie!

Sound a little ridiculous? If you're a woman and intent on living in Mexico, you'd better get used to it. Sometimes, when *piroperos* are truly inspired, they say some of the most laughable and even poetic things, such as...

"Eres una flor hermosa y fragante"
You are a beautiful and fragrant flower

"Bendita sea la madre que te parió"
Blessed be the mother who bore you!

"¡Ay, qué curvas, y yo sin frenos!"
Oh, what curves, and me without brakes!

BULLFIGHTS

Announcements of coming bullfights or *corridas de torros* are posted all over town. Entrance fees run from around $2.00 for a seat in the sun, to $6.00 for a shaded seat.

Bullfights are popular pastimes in Mexico where spectators marvel at and admire the skill and courage of the matador and the heart and stamina of the bull. Most of the fights begin around 4 p.m. The most important fights of the year take place during the winter months. Novices are featured throughout summer, spring and fall.

Less formal and less bloody are the *novilladas* or contests in which young, inexperienced men test their wits and speed against a young bull or *novillo*. These events, in which the bull is never killed, are considerably less expensive.

RECREATION

Sporting activities are abundant in Mexico but everyone lives and breaths the sport of soccer. The Mexican national team is always a tough competitor and it participated in the World Cup tournament in 1994.

Bullfights generally draw the largest number of spectators, but the fast-moving game of *jai alai* is also catching on. Basketball is immensely popular, and baseball, golf, tennis and volleyball all have their loyal followings.

Mexicans love music and dance. You'll notice that no Mexican celebration is complete without ample portions of both. Mariachi bands playing traditional ranchera music are popular with young and old. Music, food, dancing, fireworks and even bullfights are favorite ways of commemorating patron saints' days or other special occasions.

When not partying, Mexicans enjoy watching TV, listening to music and lively conversation with friends and neighbors.

SURNAMES

All Mexicans use two last names, their father's, which is always written first, and their mother's. For simplicity, the first last name is commonly used by itself, but all legal or formal documents contain both last names.

For example, in the name Gustavo Rodríguez Zapata, "Gustavo" is the man's given name, "Rodríguez" is his father's last name and the one he uses primarily, and "Zapata" is his mother's last name, used mostly on official documents.

Given the name -- Gustavo Rodríguez Zapata -- it is common for foreigners to make the mistake of calling him Mr. or *Señor* Zapata. This is incorrect. The correct form is to use the courtesy title with his *first* last name, Mr. *Rodríguez*.

Married women retain their first last name after marriage, but often substitute their husband's first last name for their own second last name. For example. When María González Jiménez marries Gustavo Rodríguez Zapata, she will often begin calling herself María González *de Rodríguez*.

Their children's last names are a combination of both the husband's and wife's. For example, Gustavo's and María's children would use the last names Rodríguez González.

Courtesy Titles When you would like to address someone respectfully, but informally, Mexicans use the courtesy titles of *Don* or *Doña* before the man or woman's given name. For example; *Don* Gustavo or *Doña* María sounds respectful, but less formal than the stodgier *Señor* Rodríguez or *Señora* González.

MEALS

Meals are very important in Mexico not only for the obvious nutrition, but also because they give families and friends a chance to socialize and catch up on the day's events.

Mexican cuisine is exquisite. Traditions vary from region to region, but some foods, such as the indispensable flour or corn-meal tortilla is ever-present. The tortilla is eaten as bread and often used as an "edible plate" to scoop up meat, chicken or vegetables. Other staples are corn, rice, beans and chiles, often combined with meat, fish or chicken and vegetables.

Frijoles refritos (refried beans) is a popular side dish, often served with *enchiladas* or flour tortillas stuffed with beef or chicken and other foods. *Enfrijoladas* are chicken-filled tortillas covered with a bean puree and cheese. *Tacos* are generally soft or crunchy tortillas filled with chicken or meat, cheese and onions. Delicious!

Be careful when ordering meals in restaurants. *Picante* means "hot" in a spicy sense, while *caliente* means a "hot" temperature. Coffee, for example, could be ordered *caliente*, but not *picante*.

After finishing a meal at a friend's house, Mexicans never leave immediately but stay around afterward to talk. On weekends, these after dinner conversations can stretch into the early hours of the morning.

Adults don't commonly eat while walking along city streets, but rather consume food purchased at street stands before continuing on their way.

TELEVISION

Foreigners feel right at home in Mexico watching channels from all over the world available through local satellite services and cable TV companies.

Satellite disks are becoming increasingly popular in Mexico. Even in smaller, rural towns, you're bound to see a large dish rising above old, run-down homes. Dish prices are dropping, but a good one will still cost from $400 to $1,000.

Cable TV service with many English-language channels is available in most large cities and towns. It is also easy to rent movies in English for the home VCR.

TIPS *Force yourself to watch Spanish language TV, at least part of the day to brush up on your language skills. Those corny U.S. sitcoms may be tempting on cable, but fight the urge! Learn the language of your new, adopted country.*

CORRUPTION AND PAYOFFS

Corruption and bribery are one of Mexico's deeply ingrained traditions that many foreigners find hard to accept. Amid layers and layers of needless bureaucracy and lack of accountability by government employees, it isn't hard to see how *La Mordida* (the bite) payoffs can flourish.

Don't be fooled, as many are, into thinking that anything can be accomplished in Mexico by slipping a few bills under the table to some greedy civil servant. These payoffs are certainly common enough, but they often blow up in the face of the person offering the bribe. Don't say we didn't warn you!

Despite tedious, time-consuming procedures that are rife with bureaucracy, it is always best to follow legal channels when applying for building permits, liquor licenses, residency and any of a plethora of other authorizations required for business and life. You're not the only one going through all these procedures. Arm yourself with patience, shrug your shoulders and take your place in line. Efforts to cut corners could end in economic disaster.

Drugs Drug corruption is a major problem in Mexico. Even the government's "drug czar," General Jesús Gutiérrez Rebollo, was arrested recently for allegedly taking money from one of the country's many drug cartels. Drug money has invaded Mexico's economy accounting for an estimated $27 billion to $30 billion yearly.

Police Many Mexicans fear the police, who they consider inept, at best. At worst, police are active participants in robberies and violent crime. Over the past three years, 27 percent of Mexico's federal police have been fired for corruption charges. Over the past year alone, more than 900 judicial police have been suspended for taking part in theft, extortion, drug trafficking and murder.

Avoid all run-ins with the police and maintain an above-board life-style. Long-time expats in Mexico have told us that they have had few problems in their infrequent encounters with police. If you go looking for problems, however, you'll probably find them.

TRAVEL WARNINGS

Arm yourself with information before heading to Mexico. The U.S. Department of State issues crime and danger fact sheets, called consular information sheets, on every country in the world.

The State Department also issues travel warnings and public announcements that you may find useful. These reports will keep you up to speed on possible cases of civil unrest, terrorist activity and other dangerous conditions, such as the breakdown of U.S. diplomatic relations. To request these reports, call (202) 647-5225, fax (202) 647-3000 or browse the Internet at http://travel.state.gov

FEDERAL BENEFITS

If you are receiving monthly benefits from Social Security, the Department of Veterans' Affairs, the Office of Personnel Management or other State or Federal office, contact the appropriate agency before leaving the U.S. to advise them of your residence abroad. They will instruct you in the procedures for having your benefit checks forwarded to you.

THE FINAL WORD

The best way to overcome the awkward feeling that newcomers always have during their first few months in Mexico, we recommend activity. Go over and introduce yourself to the neighbors. Communicate with them the best you can. If they invite you to a family function, accept. Get out of the house, join clubs, take Spanish classes and get a feel for your adopted culture. You'll feel right at home in no time.

A GRINGO'S LIFE IN A SMALL MEXICAN TOWN

With its slower pace and friendly people, an average day in a typical Mexican town can be more rewarding and less complicated than a day in the rat race back home. The following narrative describes a life style that can be enjoyed almost anywhere in Mexico.

The morning sun streams through the bedroom window. You hear your housekeeper busy preparing your desayuno of fresh-squeezed orange juice, coffee and sweet rolls, as you start getting ready to head to your bookstore in town.

Before you head out the door, you thank Renia for coming and give her her week's salary of $30.00. She'll spend the day cleaning, ironing and preparing your dinner, which she'll leave on the stove, ready to be heated when you get home tonight.

As you lock the front door, a soccer ball slams into your front gate. *"¡Perdón!"* yells a uniformed schoolboy in apology as he retrieves it and runs to get a few more kicks in before school.

You live in a *typical* Mexican small town, where a clean, comfortable, three bedroom, one bathroom home rents for $200 per month. The homes in the neighborhood are attached to the neighbors' houses on both sides and have small front yards with four-foot-high perimeter walls at a gate at the sidewalk. All windows are covered with wrought iron bars for security.

Strolling down the street to the bus stop, neighbors wave a hearty *buenos días*. The sunny, 70-degree weather makes you smile, as you remember those icy commutes to work back home. Alberto, two doors down, is finishing his new home. He was expecting to spend a total of $10,000. A local gardener, Juan Felipe, is helping him landscape the small front yard. Two streets over, a Canadian citizen, Marjorie, is building a larger, three bedroom, two-bath home for $20,000. "At those prices," you think, "it's time I pumped the $200 a month I'm paying in rent into a small home of my own."

At the bus stop at the central park or *jardín*, people were already beginning to congregate and catch up on the day's gossip. On weekends, this park will hum with activity and maybe even a mariachi band or two. The open-air market was already bustling, as shoppers fill their rickety, two-wheeled carts with fresh produce, meat, eggs, cheese and flowers.

You've come to enjoy the 10 minute bus ride into Guadalajara. Walking from the bus stop to the store, you stop by the newsstand to buy the Los Angeles Times and eye a new, corner restaurant that you'll try for lunch today — orange/guava juice, vegetable soup, beef, rice, beans and dessert for around $2.00. The two-hour lunch break will give you a chance to do a few errands.

As you weave through the corner street vendors, hawking snow cones, newspapers, fruit and other treats, you start thinking that a weekend at the beach might be nice to relax and research the possibilities of opening a seaside branch of the bookstore. The large population of foreign residents and tourists at these coastal towns could be a boon for the book business. The six-hour bus ride to the beach is comfortable in an air-conditioned, first-class passenger bus and cheap at $14.00.

As you enter your store, Señora Vargas, a neighboring shop owner, calls to you in heavily accented English, "Are you practeeesing youuur Espanish, amigo?"

"Of course!," you reply in horrendous, but improving, Spanish. "Three nights a week in class and, on Saturdays, a neighbor charges me $3.00 an hour to practice!"

You enter your store smiling, greet your assistant, Mercedes, and sit down at your desk and open the paper as the computer boots up. Another day, south-of-the-border.

WORKING FOR SALARY

Over the years we have met and interviewed hundreds of North Americans living and working in Mexico. Our informal survey tells us that around 60 percent of these people worked for salary when first arriving to the country. The majority of these people went on to start their own businesses.

Gaining knowledge of the people, developing your cross-culture skills, fine-tuning your Spanish and obtaining invaluable on-the-job experience by working for a Mexican company for a few years is the best way to settle in and get a feel for the country and live on a local budget. But don't expect to earn a lot of money. You might make a few pesos more then your Mexican counterparts, but salaries are rock-bottom by North American standards. A typical management position in Mexico pays a meager $400 to $900 U.S. per month — bare bones? Remember, Mexico's cost of living is lower too.

Katie Reeder from La Jolla, California, was just 22 years old when she came to Mexico in 1995. She first worked at a large furniture manufacturer and exporter for a year before going off on her own. After leaving the company, she worked out of her house using her prior contacts, a fax machine and a lap-top computer. She slowly built a clientele and then, with the help of an "investment angel," she was able to open her own furniture export and consultation business.

The North American Free Trade Agreement (NAFTA) makes obtaining work permits much easier for foreigners who possess unique skills that are not readily found among country nationals. Both Mexican and multinational companies are constantly seeking managers who can occupy positions of trust and responsibility — this could be the "in" you're looking for as a first-timer in Mexico.

What Mexico doesn't want, however, are unskilled workers from abroad to perform menial tasks such as bartending , retail clerking or dish washing. Thousands of Mexicans need those types of jobs to support their families and are willing to work for much less.

If you possess a unique skill, you may obtain salaried work as a conditional immigrant under the Mexican Immigration Law. These permits are granted for specific jobs. The company that hires you must contact the Immigration Department and take the legal steps to ensure you obtain your FM-3 or 2 visa (see residency section for categories of working visas). According to law, at least 90 percent of a company's employees must be Mexican nationals.

Before you head south-of-the-border seeking employment, it's a good idea to arrive in-country with a list of contacts and pre-arranged appointments. Research the foreign firms that have offices in Mexico and try to get in touch with their Stateside affiliates before you head south. Contact the American Chamber of Commerce for a list of their members or obtain the booklet, *American Firms, Subsidiaries and Affiliates — Mexico,* from the U.S. Department of Commerce in Washington D.C. Canadians can check with the nearest Mexican embassy or their own government offices.

North American companies operating in Mexico — an insurance agency, for example — need experienced U.S.-trained agents to sell their products to the local market. Mexican advertising agencies and the like also frequently seek foreign trained and educated personnel to cater to their upscale foreign clients.

Foreign attorneys may seek jobs with firms specializing in NAFTA. Or, if you have journalism experience, you can apply at one of Mexico's newspapers or magazines. Get the idea? Your special skills may land you a job that will cover your living expenses while you hunt for other opportunities. Fluency in Spanish is probably not required for many of these jobs, but it helps a lot, so hit the books.

The U.S. Peace Corps is another popular launching pad for a career in Mexico. Many volunteers use the contacts and experiences gained over their typical two-year commitment to stay in-country afterward, either working for salary or starting their own enterprise. For information on how to join the Peace Corps, call (800) 424-8580 or access the Peace Corps' website at www.peacecorps.gov.

The following are some popular work opportunities for foreigners. To perk employer interest, try publishing your name and qualifications in one of Mexico's newspapers. In-country, be sure to frequent popular expatriate hang-outs and ask the old-timers

Restaurant experience gained working for someone else can lead to successful business ventures abroad. This expat-owned pizza place in Guadalajara really packs them in.

where the job opportunities are. Most foreigners found their job simply by going to Mexico and knocking on doors, just as you would back home.

Also, check out our appendix for a list of web sites, book and magazine resources for more contacts. We've found that the bimonthly magazine *Transitions Abroad* is especially valuable for those who seek overseas work.

English teaching is a popular entry-level job among the foreign community. Language schools won't require that you speak Spanish and some won't ask for past teaching credentials. Stop by the U.S. Embassy for a list of schools.

You can acquire a teaching certificate by attending classes at some special Mexican institutions. The certificate may help you get a teaching job quicker and at better wages, but don't expect to get rich teaching English as a salaried employee. Most foreign language instructors only earn a few hundred dollars a month.

Selling time shares at one of Mexico's fine resorts is one of the best ways for a newcomer to earn good money. Skilled salespeople can earn a few thousand dollars a month, which affords a pretty good lifestyle in Mexico! To find a job, simply decide in which beach town you want to live and apply at the timeshare sales office.

House sitting jobs are usually easy to get in expat areas, since foreign home owners often leave for part of the year. Such jobs don't pay much, but at least offer room and board.

Real estate sales in expat areas is another good way to make money. You'll learn Mexico's real estate laws in no time, but remember that these jobs usually pay only commission, and it could take six months or longer to get started.

TWO WHO ARE DOIN' IT

Many expats we questioned have used their salaried job as a springboard to other opportunities. Here are a couple examples:

ALEJANDRO "ALEX" GRATTAN DOMÍNGUEZ

Alex led an exciting life as a Hollywood screenwriter and director before moving to Mexico to concentrate on his dream of writing novels. While working as editor-in-chief of a local English-language newspaper, he found time to complete the novels, *The Dark Side of the Dream* and *Breaking Even*. He's presently working on two new books.

Name:
Alejandro Grattan
Domínguez

From:
California

Residence:
Ajijic, Jalisco

Business Name:
El Ojo del Lago. He also
writes novels.

Business Description:
Editor for a small, English-
language newspaper.

How did you get started? I had written many articles before I was offered the editor's job. I was a screen writer in Hollywood for 25 years.

Why Mexico? Mexico is my mother's birthplace. I enjoy the great climate, people and scenery. I came here to write and am now working on my fifth novel.

DANA GONZALEZ

Dana, an experienced real estate saleswoman, has just started working with one of the first U.S. companies offering mortgage money to North Americans buying vacation homes or permanent residences in Mexico. She lives in Mexico with her landscape-architect husband and their three children.

Name: Dana González

From: San Luis Obispo, CA

Residence: Chapala, Jalisco

Business Name:
Inland Mortgage Corporation

Business Description: Mortgage lending for homes in Mexico to U.S. citizens and Canadians.

Why Mexico? My husband is Mexican from Chapala. We have three children and our dream was to live in Mexico, so my children and I could become bilingual and understand my husband's culture. It has been a continuous adventure. One I wouldn't trade. About 50 percent have been hard times that have made me a better person. The rest has been great, and I can now call this place home.

How did you get started? I started selling real estate in this area and did OK for a beginner. Because of my connection with real estate, Inland Mortgage Corporation approached me. I took the job because I believe we are about to see a big real estate boom, now that mortgages are available.

Key to Success: God, prayer, His word, high morals, integrity, honesty, a pioneer spirit, hard work and love for all people.

REAL ESTATE

Mexico's dedication to free trade hasn't been limited to imports and exports. The country also encourages foreign investment in all types of real estate ventures. It's a buyers' market.

Changes in the Foreign Investment Law, the implementation of the North American Free Trade Agreement (NAFTA) and the devaluation of the peso, all combine to create attractive opportunities for foreign investors to enter the real estate market now. Devaluation caused prices to fall 60 percent in 1995. Sales and rentals have both been affected as Mexican incomes were cut in half and interest rates sky-rocketed.

More than three years later, interest rates have come down and the economy is improving, but the foreign buyer can still find bargains, especially in ethnic Mexican neighborhoods. Properties in the "gringo enclaves," usually priced in dollars, have held their prices throughout the past economic crisis.

Savvy foreign real estate investors are aggressively buying up the devalued houses and apartments at bargain prices, planning to hold on to them and wait for the market to fully recover. Many of the "small investors" feel the popular tourist and expatriate living areas don't offer much return on their investment, because all the "Mexico hype" has kept prices high in the dollar-dominated neighborhoods.

For example, in the popular expat town of Ajijic, local real estate experts say home prices have either remained stable or gone up slightly over the last few years. Many foreign holders, not really needing to sell, simply took their properties off the market in the hopes of more gravy days ahead.

Fringe Areas Both new investors and seasoned real estate experts are concentrating on the fringe areas around the wealthy, gringo neighborhoods where bargains are still available in pesos. A three-bedroom home on the beach in Cancún would sell for around $400,000, while the same home some 30 miles away along the same coastline goes for only $85,000. Sound like it's worth the drive?

These fringe communities are often within easy range of golf courses, restaurants, theaters, local clubs and other haunts frequented by foreigners or upscale Mexicans.

Before signing any contract, make sure the home has access to water, electricity and telephone. If you buy intelligently in these areas, you should get a higher return on your money when the market recovers in a few years. The favorable location will also help you hedge future devaluations -- and there will be future devaluations.

Buying a home is probably one of the safest investments in the U.S. that is practically guaranteed to provide you with a high return. This isn't necessarily so in Mexico, where devaluation and volatile inflation rates are always a threat. You may wish to rent for a few years until you get a feel for the country's economic fluctuations.

RENTALS

Finding a place to live is usually a newcomer's most frustrating project. Plan to stay in an inexpensive hotel ($15/night) or rent an inexpensive apartment for a few weeks until you thoroughly research the more permanent possibilities and search for the best deal. Many beginners jump at the first bargain they find, only to discover later that even better deals were there for the taking.

A real estate agent can help you find a suitable rental, but you can do the same, at even lower prices, if you start pounding the pavement, searching for *Se Renta* or *Para Alquilar* signs and talking to local residents.

Expect to pay rent in dollars in the popular expat areas. A two-bedroom, one-bath home could rent for $400 and up. A three-bedroom, two-bath could go for $1,000 or more. Considerable savings are available in the typical Mexican neighborhoods, where you could find a two-bedroom home for $100 or a three-bedroom for less than $300.

We much prefer ethnic, Mexican neighborhoods and not only for the lower prices. Part of the beauty of living abroad is expanding your language and cultural horizons -- something that you can't easily do when surrounded by people from your homeland.

Beware! Rental homes in Mexican neighborhoods often do not include stove, refrigerator, washer or dryer. You often have to foot the bill for those amenities, as well as curtains, light bulbs and more.

Telephone service may be available upon request, but your landlord will probably require a deposit.

All these services are typically included in rentals located in expat communities, but we still feel the savings and cultural enrichment make *the barrio* the way to go, especially in the long run.

Landlord/Tenant laws top the list as Mexico's most confusing. It's a good idea to have a reputable attorney or real estate agent look over the contract before you sign, but even they will tell you that your best protection is to maintain an amiable relationship with your landlord.

CHANGING DEMOGRAPHICS

In the past, most U.S. and Canadian expatriates in Mexico were full and part-time retirees, looking to stretch their social security checks and escape the blizzards and mounting heating bills back home. But as the market continues to open, growing numbers of baby boomers are realizing the benefits of living and investing abroad.

More than 500,000 North Americans are currently dispersed throughout Mexico. The country offers almost as many climates, terrains, bustling cities and quaint colonial towns as there are foreigners who desire to relocate.

Most entrepreneurs choose locations where they can put their skills or ideas to work, often with Mexican partners or distributors.

Business people usually settle near one of the major cities such as Mexico City, Guadalajara or Monterrey. Tourism professionals often choose coastal regions along the Pacific Riviera, such as Alcapulco or Puerto Vallarta, or Cancún on the Caribbean side. Others are looking for a quiet retirement community where they can live well on a tight budget and enjoy a temperate climate and the company of other retirees. These people often choose the popular retirement communities of Lake Chapala, Ajijic, San Miguel de Allende, Cuernavaca or even the decidedly more bustling Guadalajara. Other locations, such as Cabo San Lucas or Rosarito Beach in Baja California provide all the benefits the retiree is looking for, at locations conveniently close to the U.S.

The following U.S. State Department statistics show where most U.S. citizens settle in Mexico. The figures don't reflect expat Canadians or foreigners who live in Mexico as tourists without ever seeking residency.

CITY	ESTIMATED U.S. POP.
Mexico City	350,000
Ciudad Juarez	20,247
Guadalajara	50,000
Monterrey	50,600
Tijuana	55,000
Hermosillo	6,000
Matamoros	12,000
Mérida	5,150
Nuevo Laredo	1,150

Few Mexican cities and towns are more than a two to four-hour plane flight to the U.S. Many expatriates drive back once or twice a year to visit family or friends.

CAUTION

Moving to a foreign country, learning a new language and adapting to a sometimes radically different culture is a decision that deserves a lot of consideration. It is highly advisable to spend extended vacations of two to three months or more in Mexico before finally deciding to relocate there. During that time, you can thoroughly analyze your ability to adapt to the change. Most expatriates feel that Mexico's economic advantages and friendly people far outweigh the country's drawbacks, but come down and see for yourself. Don't take our word for it.

The following nine regions are the most popular with North American expatriates. Prices here tend to be high, but in most of these cities it is possible to buy a comfortable and secure house or condominium for $20,000 to $60,000, or pay to rent for $200 to $300 per month. Use the following prices as a rough guide only.

MEXICO CITY

Population: 20 million
Altitude: 7,280 feet (2,184 meters)
Location: South-Central
Climate: Mexico City's highest temperature is around 88°F (31°C) during the April/May warm season. The rainy season from June to September is cooler with temperatures in the low 70sF (20sC). About five inches of rain will fall monthly during this season, but daily rains are generally concentrated into two or three hours each afternoon. From December to February nightly temperatures can drop to near freezing, while the days warm up to 65°F (18°C).

Housing: Housing costs in Mexico City are among the country's highest. With the recent devaluation it is possible to find some good buys and reasonable rentals:

Homes for Sale			Homes for Lease		
Luxury	*Residential*	*Medium*	*Luxury*	*Residential*	*Medium*
$500,000 & up	$150,000 - $500,000	$80,000 - $150,000	$2,500 - $10,000	$800 - $2,500	$500 - $800
Apartments for Sale			Apartments for Lease		
Luxury	*Residential*	*Medium*	*Luxury*	*Residential*	*Medium*
$250,000 & up	$100,000 - $250,000	$60,000 - $100,000	$1,000 - $5,000	$500 - $1,000	$200 - $500

Mexico City (*Distrito Federal*) is the country's fast-moving capital and the most populous city in the world. Similar to New York or London, Mexico City is the political, industrial and cultural center of the country.

Some days, air quality is among the worst in the world with ozone levels more than double the acceptable norm for large cities. The city is trying to regulate the number of cars in circulation by limiting their use two days a week during the winter months of December to February, when cold air keeps the smog layer low.

Most expatriates who live in Mexico City are business owners. Retirees usually choose less expensive, slower-paced areas with a considerably better climate and air quality.

Housing is expensive in the capital, but several attractive residential areas were made more affordable by the 1995 devaluation. These areas include the northwest district of Satélite, the Polanco area on the edge of Chapultepec Park and the Del Valle community along Insurgentes. Polanco is famous with younger executives for its upscale shopping and restaurant district. Its location closer-in to downtown shortens morning commuting time.

More exclusive areas include Lomas de Chapultepec, Herradura, Vista Hermosa, Bosques de Las Lomas and Cuajimalpa. The northwest districts of Club de Golf and Chiluca, as well as the southwest neighborhoods of San Angel Inn, Pedregal and San Jerónimo feature beautiful large homes with impressive landscaping, swimming pools and other amenities. These areas, far enough from downtown to enjoy cleaner air, are the frequent choice of foreign executives and their families.

Most expatriates choose to live outside Mexico City but return often for its many cultural attractions, entertainment, international restaurants and shopping.

GUADALAJARA

Population: 4 million
Altitude: 5,209 feet (1,563 meters)
Location: West-Central
Climate: Guadalajara has one of the country's most favor-

able climates with a year-round average temperature of 70°F (21°C). Nights are cool, usually in the 50°F (10°C) range. During the June to September rainy season, afternoon or nightly showers last two to three hours and give way to fresh, clear mornings.

Housing: Housing in Guadalajara ranges from very reasonable to very expensive. Outside the exclusive neighborhoods popular with wealthy Mexicans and expatriates, a three-bedroom home can be had for $50,000 or leased for $250.

Homes for Sale			Homes for Lease		
Luxury	Residential	Medium	Luxury	Residential	Medium
$300,000 & up	$50,000 - $300,000	$30,000 - $50,000	$2,000 - & up	$500 - $1,500	$200 - $500
Apartments for Sale			Apartments for Lease		
Luxury	Residential	Medium	Luxury	Residential	Medium
$150,000 & up	$50,000 - $150,000	$15,000 - $50,000	$1,000 & up	$400 - $800	$150 - $300

Guadalajara is Mexico's second largest city and home to the world's largest North American expat community, with some 40,000 residents.

Guadalajara is the commercial and cultural center of the country and one of the most charming, with large colonial buildings, centuries-old monuments and rose-lined boulevards. Modern skyscrapers, master-planned residential communities, upscale shopping malls and first-rate golf courses provide the city with an intricate blend of old and new.

Most industry and working-class neighborhoods are located in the southern sector of the city, while up north, middle to upper class families live suburban-style in such communities as Zapopán, close to office and shopping districts.

Areas most popular with foreigners include Lomas del Valle, Colinas de San Javier and Ciudad del Sol. The beautiful outlying areas of Santa Anita, San Isidro and Rancho Contento also provide comfortable living.

Guadalajara's large foreign population makes research and information gathering about your possible new home much easier.

The veterans here can fill newcomers in on life in Mexico and is a must-stop for anyone considering relocating.

Popular expatriate clubs and hang-outs include the American Society of Jalisco at telephone 621-2395, Sandi's Bookstore at 121-0863 and the Fran Furton Seminar held Tuesday mornings, telephone 121-2348. Those seeking business opportunities should contact the American Chamber of Commerce of Mexico in Guadalajara at telephone 634-6606.

LAKE CHAPALA AND AJIJIC

Population: 60,000
Altitude: 5,000 feet (1,500 meters)
Location: West-Central
Climate: The climate in Chapala and Ajijic is very similar to Guadalajara. The lake helps keep the overall temperature slightly cooler in summer and slightly warmer in winter. During the June to September rainy season, showers fall at night and give way to fresh, clear mornings.
Housing: Only 35 minutes from Guadalajara on Mexico's largest lake, the towns of Chapala, Ajijic, Chula Vista and Jocotepec are home to the country's most concentrated foreign population. Housing prices and leases are moderate to expensive.

Homes for Sale			Homes for Lease		
Luxury	Residential	Medium	Luxury	Residential	Medium
$300,000 & up	$80,000 - $300,000	$40,000 - $80,000	$2,000 - & up	$500 - $1,500	$250 - $500
Apartments for Sale			Apartments for Lease		
Luxury	Residential	Medium	Luxury	Residential	Medium
$100,000 & up	$60,000 - $100,000	$30,000 - $60,000	$1,000 & up	$400 - $1,000	$150 - $400

Besides near-perfect weather conditions, this region offers the best array of foreign social activities and entertainment options in the country. Latin America's largest American Foreign Legion post is located in Chapala. Bridge and garden clubs abound, as well as other organized activities such as Lions Club, the Lakeside

Little Theatre group, Masons and Memorial Society. The region also features golf courses, tennis courts and hot mineral springs.

The Chapala Society in Ajijic hosts the largest English language book library in the region. Once an avant garde community of Mexican and foreign artists, the town is now a fashionable residential district with upscale restaurants and boutiques.

Beverly Hunt, owner of the Laguna Real Estate Company (Tel. 376-6-1186), or David Merryman, owner of REMAX Lake Chapala (Tel. 376-6-1511) are well-qualified to answer any questions about land, housing or rentals in the region. Beverly also owns a quaint bed and breakfast where visitors will probably run into other future expatriates seeking information about everything from residency to acquiring a Mexican drivers license.

While in Chapala, be sure to stop by and talk with "Mago," who is an expert at obtaining everything from residency credentials, telephone service and drivers licenses. Her fees are reasonable and her service is undoubtedly much faster than most attorneys. Give Mago a call at 376-5-4199.

MONTERREY

Population: 3.5 million
Altitude: 1,800 feet (540 meters)
Location: Northeast, 145 miles from Texas border
Climate: Settled at the foot of the Sierra Madre mountains, 80°F (27°C) or hotter temperatures are common from April through October. During the winter months, from December through February, nights can be chilly to cold. Rain falls here only in August and September.
Housing: Few people live directly in Monterrey, but rather in surrounding suburbs, and rely heavily on their automobile for transport to work, school or shopping. Colonia del Valle is one of the city's quality residential areas. Others, called "colonias," include Fuentes del Valle, Santa Engrancia and San Augustín. Other popular areas are San Patricio, Bosques del Valle and Del Rosario. Life here is faster, and housing prices are economical to expensive.

Homes for Sale			Homes for Lease		
Luxury	Residential	Medium	Luxury	Residential	Medium
$400,000 & up	$50,000 - $350,000	$30,000 - $50,000	$2,000 - & up	$500 - $1,500	$200 - $500
Apartments for Sale			Apartments for Lease		
Luxury	Residential	Medium	Luxury	Residential	Medium
$150,000 & up	$60,000 - $150,000	$20,000 - $60,000	$2,000 & up	$400 - $1,000	$150 - $400

Monterrey is Mexico's third largest city and industrial capital. This important northern city is home to four universities, five small colleges and more than 70 trade schools. The pace here differs from the country's southern colonial towns.

Its strategic location only 145 miles from the Texas border helps make it the country's prime financial center. More than half the banking industry is located here.

Excellent highways connect this sprawling city with the U.S. to the north and to all southern Mexico's business centers and towns. The excellent transport infrastructure has made Monterrey the country's hub of industry for textiles, furniture, cement, steel, tile and chemicals.

Long recognized for its industrial strength, the city has concentrated its recent efforts toward improving cultural life. The local government is seeking to develop the city's many museums, historical sites, fairs and other attractions.

SAN MIGUEL DE ALLENDE

Population: 55,000
Altitude: 6,134 feet (1,840 meters)
Location: Central
Climate: San Miguel has a wonderfully stable climate with year-round temperatures that range from 57° to 75°F (14° to 24°C). The rainy season runs from July to September. The driest months are typically March and April.
Housing: Numerous planned subdivisions unite retired North Americans and wealthy Mexicans to spend vacations in their

San Miguel summer homes. Housing prices are economical to expensive.

Homes for Sale			Homes for Lease		
Luxury	Residential	Medium	Luxury	Residential	Medium
$300,000 & up	$60,000 - $200,000	$30,000 - $60,000	$3,000 - & up	$500 - $1,500	$200 - $500
Apartments for Sale			Apartments for Lease		
Luxury	Residential	Medium	Luxury	Residential	Medium
$150,000 & up	$40,000 - $80,000	$15,000 - $40,000	$1,000 & up	$300 - $1,000	$150 - $300

About three hours northwest of the capital, San Miguel de Allende is a picture-postcard Mexican colonial city. More than 3,000 North American expatriates call San Miguel home for at least part of the year. The town is known for its beautifully restored colonial houses that line cobblestone streets. Scores of fashionable boutiques, fine restaurants and quaint parks of century-old churches make the region popular with tourists as well as expatriates.

The community is perhaps best known as the home of Instituto Allende, one of Latin America's top schools of fine arts for English-speaking students. For more than 40 years, foreign students have come here to study, but then fall in love with the quiet colonial atmosphere and decide to make San Miguel home.

PUERTO VALLARTA

Population: 300,000
Altitude: Sea level
Location:: Central Pacific Coast
Climate: During the July and August summer months as much as four inches (10 cm) of rain could fall per month. Temperatures remain almost a constant 75°F (24°C) year-round, but summer warming trends do occur.
Housing: Numerous new and established developments are located north and south of Puerto Vallarta. One region popular with expatriates is known locally as "gringo gulch," where

numerous foreigners live full-time, or come down several months a year to avoid northern winters. Housing here is expensive.

Homes for Sale			Homes for Lease		
Luxury	Residential	Medium	Luxury	Residential	Medium
$800,000 & up	$200,000 - $500,000	$100,000 - $200,000	$4,000 - & up	$1,500 - $3,000	$500 - $1,500
Apartments for Sale			Apartments for Lease		
Luxury	Residential	Medium	Luxury	Residential	Medium
$300,000 & up	$100,000 - $200,000	$40,000 - $80,000	$2,000 & up	$800 - $1,500	$200 - $800

Puerto Vallarta was still a sleepy fishing village in 1954 when Aeromexico began sending daily flights from Guadalajara. The village was a natural tourist destination for residents of Mexico's second largest city.

Cobblestone streets, red-tile roofs and quaint shops and restaurants give Puerto Vallarta a lingering colonial feel that conceals the luxury beach resort it is. The year-round warm climate and picturesque, colonial setting attract many full-time foreign residents looking for a small town atmosphere with big city amenities.

Over the past 10 years, much of the community's real estate has been developed into large planned communities with marinas, residential and commercial zones and tourist facilities.

Several mega-developments are situated around the Bahía de Banderas, the largest natural bay in Mexico. One such development is the Marina Vallarta, a 445-acre planned community that includes the country's largest marina. Nuevo Vallarta, located eight miles north of town, is a 1,150-acre community with golf course, marina, shopping facilities, homesites and an exclusive health spa.

Closer to town, picturesque hillside mansions sell from $300,000 to $7 million, and small condo's start at $65,000. Downtown, fixer-uppers with a colonial flare start at $100,000, and a small condo will fetch $40,000.

Expatriates who don't desire a full-time beach lifestyle will often choose to live in Guadalajara, just five hours inland, and travel to Puerto Vallarta for periodic vacations.

CUERNAVACA

Population: 500,000
Altitude: 5,000 feet (1,500 meters)
Location: Central
Climate: Located just south of Mexico City, the climate in
Cuernavaca is similar to the nation's capital, but without the
noise, smog and agitation of the big city. Year-round tem-
peratures hover around 70°F (21°C), but drop considerably at
night, especially during the December to February winter
months. Rainy season runs from June through September. Like
Mexico City, rains fall for a few hours in the late afternoon,
giving rise to a fresh, cool sunrise the following day.
Housing: Cuernavaca has been viewed as a retirement or
vacation spot from ancient Aztec times. Indian ruler
Moctezuma, Spanish conquistador Hernán Cortéz and the
Emperor Maximilian all took refuge in the region's natural
springs and bountiful forests. Known for its beautiful homes,
surrounded by high walls, the city is today's refuge for retired
politicians, entrepreneurs and Mexico City's elite. Housing is
moderate to expensive.

Homes for Sale			Homes for Lease		
Luxury	Residential	Medium	Luxury	Residential	Medium
$300,000 & up	$70,000 - $300,000	$30,000 - $70,000	$3,000 - & up	$500 - $2,000	$200 - $500
Apartments for Sale			Apartments for Lease		
Luxury	Residential	Medium	Luxury	Residential	Medium
$100,000 & up	$60,000 - $100,000	$15,000 - $50,000	$2,000 & up	$400 - $1,000	$150 - $400

Famous for the 470-year-old Palace of Cortés, which features a colorful mural depicting the nation's history by famous
Mexican painter Diego Rivera, Cuernavaca has developed as a
popular retirement region and bedroom community for those wishing to escape the hustle and bustle of the capital.
Its attractive shops are filled with local handicrafts, but nearby

department stores and modern grocery stores and a proliferation of English-language publications, reveal the community's quiet sophistication.

Many clubs and social activities cater to the expatriate, including the Navy League of the United States, the American Legion and other organizations. Newcomers find in these groups important contacts among the English-speaking retirement community.

CANCÚN

Population: 250,000
Altitude: Sea level
Location: On the tip of the Yucatán Peninsula.
Climate: Average year-round temperatures hover in the 80°F (27°C) range. Summer months of April and May are hot and humid with frequent but brief showers. The region receives less rainfall than the U.S. Virgin Islands, Bahamas and many Caribbean destinations. Cancún has been generally unaffected by seasonal tropical storms in the Gulf of Mexico. It recovered quickly from Hurricane Gilbert in 1988 — the first hurricane to hit Cancún in 50 years.
Housing: Tourism is booming in Cancún, but the average expatriate often chooses more economical off-the-beach locations to set up a permanent residence here. Downtown Cancún now offers many small, comfortable-looking houses for those who aren't satisfied to just pass through. Nearby Cozumel Island or Playa del Carmen offer beautiful, reasonably priced condo's. Both are located 35 miles south of Cancún along an excellent freeway.

Homes for Sale			Homes for Lease		
Luxury	Residential	Medium	Luxury	Residential	Medium
$500,000 & up	$200,000 - $500,000	$80,000 - $200,000	$4,000 - & up	$1,000 - $4,000	$400 - $1,000
Apartments for Sale			Apartments for Lease		
Luxury	Residential	Medium	Luxury	Residential	Medium
$300,000 & up	$100,000 - $200,000	$40,000 - $100,000	$2,000 & up	$800 - $1,500	$300 - $800

At 12 miles long and a quarter mile wide, Cancún is sometimes considered a large sandbar rather than an island. It was born and developed as a resort town in the 1970s. Some say it may be the world's first completely planned resort community. Downtown Cancún is a monument to the world's finest resort hotels. The island's sparkling green/blue waters have attracted divers and sun lovers from all over the world, and its limestone-based porous white sand is comfortable to walk or lie on even during the hottest months. It is also located conveniently close to the famous Mayan ruins of Chichen Itza. Often called Mexico's premier resort, Cancún is a short hour-and-a-half plane ride from Mexico City, and is even nearer to southern Florida.

CABO SAN LUCAS AND SAN JOSÉ DEL CABO

Population: 65,000
Altitude: Sea level
Location: Tip of the Baja California Peninsula
Climate: Dry almost year-round, with 300 days of sunshine per year and average temperatures of 75°F (24°C).
Housing: Many foreign residents have settled in Cabo San Lucas and San José del Cabo in recent years. Popular expatriate developments include El Pedregal de San Lucas, Misiones del Cabo, Cabo Bello, Punta Palmilla, La Jolla, Gringo Hill, Acapulquito and Costa Azul.

Homes for Sale			Homes for Lease		
Luxury	*Residential*	*Medium*	*Luxury*	*Residential*	*Medium*
$500,000 & up	$100,000 - $300,000	$50,000 - $80,000	$2,000 - & up	$800 - $2,000	$350 - $500
Apartments for Sale			**Apartments for Lease**		
Luxury	*Residential*	*Medium*	*Luxury*	*Residential*	*Medium*
$100,000 & up	$60,000 - $100,000	$30,000 - $60,000	$1,500 & up	$400 - $1,000	$200 - $400

The transpeninsular highway from La Paz to Cabo San Lucas opened up more than 1,000 miles of fascinating desert landscape and spectacular secluded beaches that once only catered to wealthy deep sea anglers who arrived in their own planes or yachts.

Today a popular cruise ship destination along the "Mexican Riviera," Cabo San Lucas and San José del Cabo, known collectively as "Los Cabos," are the site of a budding resort and expatriate community.

Mexicana, Alaska Airlines, Aero California, Continental and America West provide daily service to major U.S. destinations from the Los Cabos airport, located seven miles north of San José del Cabo.

A mecca for deep-sea anglers, divers, and water-sports fanatics, the Los Cabos region now has a host of small boutiques and shopping malls featuring a variety of casual clothing, handicrafts, jewelry, antiques and souvenirs. World-class resorts and restaurants are springing up everywhere. San José's beautiful golf course attracts enthusiasts, but also anchors a popular upscale residential district.

The region along the freeway from Cabo San Lucas to San José del Cabo is ripe with new construction. Many wealthy foreigners are buying lots and constructing in the new Punta Gorda and La Playita subdivisions to the east which, although more remote, will soon be serviced with good roads and shopping areas.

Buy or Build? The cost of building a home in Mexico ranges from $30 to $50 per square foot, depending on the amenities. If you're willing to live Mexican-style, you could build an 800 square foot, three-bedroom, one-bath home on a small, 2,000 square foot lot for around $13,000!

TIPS FOR A GOOD BUY

When purchasing real estate in Mexico or any other country, it is important to fully understand the laws and government requirements to buy or build

As a first step, choose a lawyer/notary who comes highly recommended by organizations such as the American Chamber of Commerce (AmCham), the U.S. Embassy or a reliable friend. Never rely on "professionals" recommended by the seller of the property. Keep the following in mind.

1. Send a Mexican

Send a Mexican friend into an area to research prices and availability of property. Pay a reliable, bilingual Mexican if you have to. Often, if the seller thinks he or she is dealing with a native, the price offered will be closer to the range of a more modest national salary.

2. Don't rely on advertisements

Personal research is very important to be assured the best land for the best price. Mexicans don't advertise much. Go to your area of interest and ask around. Visit the local *mercados* or small grocery stores and check their bulletin boards. Those who frequent these stores will know if anyone in town is considering selling. Talk to as many people as you can before you make an offer. The more information you have, the better you'll be able to haggle.

3. Expect to haggle

Mexicans love to haggle. Many times the land up for sale has been in their families for generations. Never be in a hurry when it comes to real estate. Make an offer and wait a while. If the land still hasn't sold, make another offer. If the owner really wants to sell, he or she will be willing to negotiate.

4. Negotiate in pesos, not dollars

If possible, do all negotiating in pesos, the national currency. Sometimes you can ask the seller to give you a fixed amount of time to pay for the property. If you set the sale price in pesos, you'll come out ahead over time as the peso devalues.

5. Beware of local labor laws

In some cases, all employees of the previous owner, including maids, gardeners and caretakers, become the responsibility of the new owner. Other liabilities could also include fines or back wages.

6. Telephone lines

Telephone lines are hard to come by in Mexico, so it's best to negotiate the purchase of the phone line with the house.

FOREIGN OWNERSHIP

In 1989 the Mexican government amended the Foreign Investment Law to allow direct foreign ownership in real estate in all but "restricted zones" regardless of the holder's legal status.

The "restricted zone," referred to as Constitutional Article 27, encompasses all land that is within 100 kilometers (62 miles) of any Mexican border and 50 kilometers (31 miles) of any Mexican coastline. With few exceptions, foreign investors seeking to own property within a restricted zone may do so only by forming a "fideicomiso" or real estate trust.

Foreign buyers purchasing property in their own name must obtain a document known as the CLAVO from the Ministry of Foreign Affairs (*Secretaría de Relaciones Exteriores*). Through this document, the foreign buyer confirms that he or she will not seek the diplomatic protection or intervention of the home country in matters pertaining to the property purchased and that he/she will agree to be subject to the Mexican legal system — as would any Mexican citizen — in all matters concerning the property.

How the Trust Works Foreigners who wish to own property within one of the country's "restricted zones" must create a 50-year renewable real estate trust or "fideicomiso." This provision was created by the Mexican government to attract foreign investors to restricted zones. This arrangement enables the investor to enjoy unrestricted use of the land as beneficiary of the trust.

Under the fideicomiso, fee simple title is placed in the name of a bank selected as trustee by the buyer. The bank then administers the property according to the buyer's instructions. The buyer/beneficiary has full ownership rights to build on the property, tear down or modify existing buildings, rent, lease or sell at any time, conforming only to Mexican general laws established for all people.

The fideicomiso is essentially a contractual agreement that in most respects is identical to the type of trust commonly used in the United States. The trust is created for 50 years and can be renewed. Title to the property may rest in one beneficiary indefinitely, provided it is renewed within the terms established by law.

How to Set Up a Trust To establish a fideicomiso, an application must be delivered to the Ministry of Foreign Relations that includes a description of the property, its intended use and personal data about each of the beneficiaries. Once granted, the bank instructs a notary to draw up the trust document, which is recorded in the state where the property is located. The bank will charge a $400 to $800 acceptance fee to set up the trust.

The beneficiary of the trust must pay a yearly fee of approximately 1 percent of the bank-appraised value of the property, or a minimum of $250 to $3,300.

The beneficiary can name a substitute beneficiary to transfer titles in case of divorce or death. This is a simple procedure that eliminates the title transfer tax, as well as the time and expense of probation.

Exception to the Restricted Zone Law Foreign investors may purchase land within a restricted zone without creating the trust, only when the land will be used for industrial, commercial or tourism activities.

Mysterious-looking walls that line colonial streets conceal immaculately landscaped gardens with fountains.

The acquisition must be registered with the Ministry of Foreign Affairs. Without forming a trust, residential use of land in restricted zones is prohibited.

Property Registration Title insurance is not available in Mexico. Some U.S. insurance companies will cover Mexican properties, but these policies are very rare. In the absence of title insurance, Mexico does have a safe form of title registration that protects the buyer from fraud and hidden claims. Most foreign buyers rely on the Mexican system.

First, an attorney conducts a title search to obtain a *certificado de libertad de gravamen*, declaring the property free from liens and encumbrances. The document is not an iron-clad guarantee, but it does offer some protection and reveals the property's current owner.

The final step toward ensuring correct registration is to obtain the property's "escritura," similar to the deed.

Escritura -vs- Deed In Mexico, property is transferred from one party to another by means of a document called an "escritura." The escritura is similar to a deed, but there are some important differences.

The original document is not given to the purchaser, but is inscribed in the notary's ledger. The buyer and seller are given copies of the original ledger entry. The copy, whether hand-written or typed, must be issued on official notarial paper. Photocopies of the document must be authenticated with a raised, notarial seal, as well as the notary's signature and information on the entry of the original transaction in the notarial ledger.

Be careful to verify all information in the escritura prior to its entry into the ledger. Correcting inaccuracies and misspellings at a later date may require a second payment of title transfer costs.

Financing Foreigners can obtain mortgage loans from a Mexican bank only if they hold permanent or temporary immigrant visas (see Residency section). However, no local financing is available at economically feasible rates. Recently, some North

American mortgage companies have entered the market offering financing for up to 70 percent of the appraised value. Interest rates vary between 2 percent and 3 percent above the prevailing U.S. rate for amortization terms of up to 20 years.

Banks will lend for primary residence and vacation homes valued between $30,000 and $500,000. Inland Mortgage Corporation (Tel: 800-585-1984 U.S.) is a leader in Mexican mortgages. A few other big names include Collateral International, Metrociti Corp., and International Mortgage Resource Corp.

These new companies are providing foreigners with exciting new possibilities for owning a home in Mexico. In the past, foreign home seekers paid in cash.

Some firms require an application fee of 1.5 percent, while others ask for a flat $250 registration fee. Mortgage documents are signed in the U.S. or Canada, and the promise to pay is considered to have originated there for legal purposes. Documentation is in English, but all Mexican transactions must be done in Spanish.

If the transaction is not paid in full, sometimes the seller will agree to a "reserve title and instalment sales contract." In this case, the buyer is considered the conditional owner of the property, as long as he or she complies with the conditions of the agreement. Title to the property is transferred to the buyer upon full payment.

To ensure the payments are made to the property owner by the buyer, it is best to place a lien on property owned by the buyer in the United States. Setting up the deal this way might be more complicated, but at least the seller does not have to return to Mexico to litigate if the purchaser defaults on the payments.

Closing Costs Closing costs and transfer taxes are determined by whichever is greater, the bank appraisal or the selling price. Since the bank appraisal is almost always the smaller amount, most buyers keep the selling price secret to avoid paying higher taxes. As a general rule, the seller pays the capital gains tax, and the buyer pays the closing cost.

Properties valued at $100,000 usually pay a closing cost of between 5 and 8 percent of the total. Less expensive properties pay a higher percentage, while higher priced properties will be less. A standard transfer should be completed 45 to 60 days from the time all documents are consummated.

The following table is a breakdown of common real estate transfer taxes and fees, how much they run and who normally pays them:

Expense	Amount	Who Pays
Certificates of no encumbrances and tax lien	$200 to $300	Buyer
Notary fees	$500 to $1,500	50/50
Filing fee, Public Registry	$100 to $300	Buyer
Appraisal fee	$200 to $500	Negotiable
Acquisition tax	2% of sale price	Buyer
Income tax	34% of the gain or 20% of the sale price	Seller
Broker's fee	5% to 6%	Seller

Earnest Money and Escrow Companies Mexico does not have escrow companies that handle the buyer's deposit while he or she is conducting studies of property under the terms of the contract. Rather than have the seller, attorney or real estate agent hold the deposit during this process, it is advisable to work with an escrow company in the United States that will carry out all the instructions of the purchase contract.

ATTORNEYS AND NOTARIES

A Mexican attorney should draw up the real estate contract and review all its conditions and terms. A notary is also a licensed attorney, but is issued a special license to act as an extension of the government to ensure all real estate transactions are executed according to the law. A document signed by a notary is a legally binding, valid document.

It is important to note that the notary is not obligated to advise either party regarding legal options available to them, such as tax consequences or who is responsible for closing costs. It's a good idea to do extensive research yourself to become aware of the options before conducting a real estate transaction in Mexico.

CAPITAL GAINS

Capital gains tax is based on 34 percent of the sales gain, or 20 percent of the sale price. Foreigners who can prove at least two years legal residence with FM-2 or FM-3 status will not be subject to capital gains on the sale of their Mexican home.

Additional proof, such as two years' receipts for gas, telephone and electricity services in the party's name may also be required to avoid capital gains. Save your receipts!

EJIDO PROPERTY

In the past, some rural land was put aside for peasant farmers to help bring about an equitable distribution of property. This land was called "ejido" property to which the peasants had limited title. The peasant could not sell the land or use it as collateral. If he didn't continue to work the land, the title would be revoked.

Changes to the Constitution and the new Agrarian Law now permits peasants to own, and therefore sell, the land granted them under the old law. This revision has opened the door to foreigners wishing to buy rural inland or coastal properties that were once off limits. When considering the purchase of ejido property, an attorney or reliable real estate agent should thoroughly research the transaction to be sure the seller has conformed to all selling laws.

REAL ESTATE AGENTS

The only accredited, professional real estate organization in Mexico is the Mexican Association of Real Estate Professionals

(AMPI), or the "Asociación Mexicana de Profesionales Inmobiliarios, A.C." AMPI is similar to the U.S. Association of Realtors and has 33 chapters nation wide.

Real estate agencies are not regulated by Mexican law. Agents are not required to have licenses, although such legislation is currently under consideration. Property owners, managers and leasing or sales agents can operate regardless of their technical capacities. For this reason, prices and conditions vary in Mexico depending on whom you deal with.

Always seek professional assistance when purchasing real estate in Mexico. Although not regulated by law, many agencies comply with AMPI's strict code of ethics. Some agents specialize in specific services, such as types of properties, regional areas or building class.

HOME OWNERS INSURANCE

Mexican home owners insurance policies cover homes, apartments or condo's and their contents against damage from fire, theft, vandalism, explosions, winds, hurricanes and even earthquakes. Protection is extended to third parties, such as visitors, maids, repair technicians or others who may be injured while in your residence.

Protection is even available against civil law claims resulting from damages or injuries caused to others while you or members of your family engage in non-professional sports such as golf, hunting, fishing, swimming, bowling or boating.

CURRENCY LAW AND CONTRACTS IN SPANISH

Real estate contracts may be drawn up in English but must subsequently be translated into Spanish to be acceptable in court. Contracts may be drawn-up in foreign currency. The buyer may pay the contract's equivalent in pesos at the current rate of exchange on the day the payment is due.

TIME SHARES

Proceed with caution here. North Americans who become involved in time-share purchases should be aware that Mexican laws and practices are markedly different from those in the U.S. Foreigners purchasing time shares in Mexico do not have much protection under Mexican law and should be aware of the high risks involved.

All contracts must be executed in Mexican pesos to be valid. If payment for the contract is made by credit card, the ultimate price of the contract negotiated in U.S. dollars may vary from the rate discussed.

WATER AND GAS

Water pressure is low in most of Mexico, so many homes have an underground cistern, called an *aljibe*, from which the water is pumped to a tank, or *tinaco*, on the roof. Gravity then carries the water down to the sinks, toilets and showers. This measure is used when city water pressure is insufficient. Be sure your rental home has a cistern and pump. A spare pump is also recommendable for emergencies.

All cooking and water heating in Mexico is done by butane gas, either stored in portable cylinders or in a stationary tank. Most residents prefer the stationary tank, which the gas company comes and fills regularly. The monthly gas bill for a three-bedroom home runs around $25.

THE FINAL WORD

Devaluation Most foreigners buy real estate in Mexico as an investment, as well as a place to enjoy the good life. As an investment, you always hope to make more in Mexico that you would on a similar investment in the U.S. or Canada, but to do so, it is imperative that you fully understand how the devaluation of the peso can affect your return on an investment. This is called dual currency economics.

When you buy real estate with dollars in Mexico, it is immediately invested in a peso denominated economy. Your dollar is converted into the peso until it is withdrawn and converted back into dollars.

Inflation substantially influences the transaction, as does the rate of exchange. As a result, your investment in Mexico is subject to two independent inflation rates: your country's rate and Mexico's rate.

The appreciation potential of any investment will be influenced by factors mentioned above: devaluation of the peso, inflation rate in Mexico and the inflation rate back home.

These factors won't affect you, however, if you simply live with pesos and don't convert them into dollars, or if you buy and sell in areas like Lake Chapala, where most transactions are done in dollars.

HEALTH OPTIONS

"**D**on't drink the water!" Those four words have become synonymous over the years with vacations in Mexico. But first-time visitors are often surprised to learn that the dreaded nausea and diarrhea of "Montezuma's Revenge" is more a phenomenon among uninformed tourists than among seasoned residents.

"The Revenge," more aptly named *turista* by the Mexicans, is usually caused by consumption of contaminated food, ice or tap water. Sitting around in the local bars, we have seen many cases in the making.

Recently arrived tourists are cautious of Mexico's notoriously bad tap water, but as the vacation wares on, they begin chugging down the country's infamous margaritas and double shotting Cuervo Gold tequila. They sample a tasty-looking taco from a street vendor -- something seasoned residents rarely do --and become overly confident with water, using it, despite the warnings in their tourist book, to brush their teeth. That's when Montezuma arrives to lay down the law.

Caution with impure water and untreated foods, like raw fruits and vegetables, becomes second nature to the resident of Mexico. Can you brush your teeth with tap water? What about that water that accidently trickles down your throat as you take a shower? What are the limits?

You will soon discover that water quality depends on where

you are in the country and what types of establishments you frequent. In Tijuana, even the old-time Mexicans won't drink, or even brush their teeth using tap water. In certain areas like Cancún or Cabo, some people drink the tap water, but beware! As a general rule, water is undrinkable all over Mexico. Smart newcomers learn the limits by talking with the locals and the long-time expats. Most aren't fanatical, but do take precautions.

KEEPING MONTEZUMA AT BAY

Bottled drinking water can be delivered to your home or purchased in the local supermarket. Untreated milk and dairy products and uncooked fruits and vegetables should be avoided. Food and drink in most tourist-frequented restaurants is generally safe, as are pasteurized milk sold in disposable cartons, beer and soft drinks. Don't drink or eat anything, including ice, if you're unsure about sanitary conditions. Always ask.

Fruits and vegetables washed with tap water should also be disinfected. Disinfectant drops are sold in the produce section of local supermarkets.

Water Water that has been adequately chlorinated using systems similar to those of the U.S. will afford significant protection against viral and bacterial waterborne diseases. However, chlorine treatment alone, as used in routine disinfection of water, may not kill some parasitic organisms that cause giardiasis, amebiasis and cryptosporidiosis (i.e. nasty stuff). In areas where chlorinated tap water is not available or where hygiene and sanitation are poor, only beer, wine, bottled beverages and soft drinks or beverages made with boiled water, such as tea or coffee, may be safe to drink.

Mexican law requires that ice be made from purified water, but don't get too confident. If the water in an establishment is contaminated, the ice is too, so be careful! If ice has been in contact with containers used for drinking, the containers should be thoroughly cleaned, preferably with soap and hot water, after the ice has been discarded.

It is safer to drink directly from a can or bottle than from a questionable container, i.e. a glass that has been washed with contaminated water. Wet cans or bottles should be dried before being opened, and surfaces which come in contact with the mouth should be wiped clean. In areas notorious for impurities, don't brush your teeth using tap water.

WATER TREATMENT

Boiling is by far the most reliable method of purifying water. Bring the water to a vigorous, rolling boil for one minute and allow it to cool to room temperature. Do not add ice, unless it was made with purified water. At altitudes above 6,562 feet (2 km.), boil for three minutes or use chemical disinfection. Adding a pinch of salt to each quart, or pouring the water several times from one container to another will improve the taste.

Chemical disinfection with iodine is an alternative method of water treatment, when boiling is unfeasible. Disinfection is commonly achieved through the use of a tincture of iodine or of tetraglycine hydroperiodide tablets, both available at pharmacies and supermarkets.

Follow the manufacturer's instructions. If the water is cloudy, the number of tablets should be doubled. Attempt to warm water that is very cold before adding iodine.

A variety of portable, iodine-impregnated filters are currently on the market that claim to instantly provide potable water, but no clinical study has ever proven that they are 100 percent effective. Conventional water purification methods are better.

If no safe drinking water is available or can be obtained, tap water that is uncomfortably hot to touch may be safer than cold tap water, but proper disinfection is still advised.

Food Select all foods with care, particularly in areas where hygiene and sanitation are inadequate. Avoid salads, uncooked vegetables, unpasteurized milk and milk products, such as cheese. Eat cooked foods while they are still hot, and peel fruits and vegetables before eating. Eating food prepared by a street vendor is like giving Montezuma an open invitation to come calling.

Babies up to 6 months should stick to breast feeding or risk their own bout with "The Revenge."

Fish and shellfish can contain poisonous biotoxins, even when well-cooked. Barracuda, red snapper, grouper, amberjack, sea bass and a wide range of tropical reef fish are common in local restaurants, but should be avoided.

PREVENT TRAVELERS' DIARRHEA

Travelers' Medical Alert to Mexico, by Dr. William Forgey, is your best defense against travelers' diarrhea in Mexico. Forgey cites a study of U.S. residents in Guadalajara, which shows that taking two Pepto Bismol tablets four times daily with meals and at bedtime decreases the incidence of travelers' diarrhea from 61 to 23 percent. This dosage may be taken for up to three weeks. Products containing aspirin should not be taken concurrently. This sounds more like a preventive method used by travelers, rather than a "cure" for diarrhea for Mexican residents.

Dr. Forgey also states that the most effective remedy for diarrhea to date is Imodium (loperamide) and the prescription antibiotic Bactrim DS. These remedies have alleviated nearly 100 percent of cramping and runny stools within one hour. Dosages are described in the package inserts for both medications. Check with your physician concerning the use of these products and a prescription.

MALARIA

Severe diarrhea caused by contaminated food and drink is the most frequently reported illness among travelers in Mexico. In some very rural, Pacific and Gulf Coast areas, the possibility also exists of contracting malaria. All tourist areas are free of malaria, as are urban areas.

Malaria is a serious parasitic infection transmitted by a mosquito that usually bites from dusk to dawn. Symptoms are flu-like: fever, chills, general achiness and tiredness.

In infested areas, use a mosquito net over the bed, apply insect repellent to skin and clothing and avoid outdoor activities after dusk. Risk of malaria exists only below the 1,000-meter level.

Before traveling, check with the U.S. embassy for updated

travelers' heath advisories to Mexico, or contact the Center for Disease Control hotline at (404) 332-4559.

HEALTH CARE IN MEXICO

Medical and dental care in Mexico is adequate and affordable. Mexico City and Guadalajara are home to some of the best health care services in Latin America.

Mexico's health care system consists of a public and a private sector. On the public side, the Mexican Institute of Social Security (IMSS) operates about 20 percent of the country's 3,000 hospitals and clinics, serving 60 million Mexicans, or roughly 70 percent of the population. Small private hospitals — which average about 12 beds each — provide about half of Mexico's operating rooms, serving around 20 million wealthy Mexicans. The remaining 10 million people are uninsured and subject to typically dehumanizing treatment at the State clinics, known as *"hospitales generales."*

Foreigners are eligible to apply for the country's low-cost National Health Insurance that covers a broad range of medical services. Many Mexican doctors and dentists speak English and have either been trained in the U.S. or attend regular classes there to learn the latest techniques.

Mexico's proximity to the U.S. provides expatriates with an added benefit not readily enjoyed by foreign residents of more distant countries — the possibility of returning to the U.S. for complicated procedures. Mexican doctors will regularly refer their patients to U.S. hospitals if the technology is unavailable in-country.

PHARMACIES

Mexico is the base for most of the world's major pharmaceutical manufacturing companies. Pharmacies here are well-stocked with all the most necessary prescription drugs at prices far below those of their U.S. counterparts.

A 1992 study revealed that U.S. medical costs are three times higher than medical costs in Mexico, where brand-name drugs can be up to five times less expensive. With the 1994 peso devaluation, price differences today are even greater.

A month's supply of a popular birth control pill made by Wyeth Laboratories costs $24.00 in California. The same pills cost $1.31 in Los Algodones, Mexico, at the current exchange rate.

Why the big difference? Mexico's lower standard of living has obligated the U.S. pharmaceutical companies to sell their wares at prices far below domestic ones. Also, the Mexican government is permitted, under the North American Free Trade Agreement (NAFTA) to heavily subsidize and control the prices of certain drugs.

Most drugs sold in Mexico are identical to their U.S. counterparts, often manufactured by the same laboratory, and are available without a prescription.

A doctor's prescription is not required for many drugs like penicillin, ampicillin and most pain killers. However, a recent law aimed at curbing the widespread practice of self-medicating has outlawed the non-prescription use of sleeping pills, morphine, narcotics and other mind-altering drugs. A U.S. citizen is currently in jail in Tijuana facing a 25-year term for buying medications with the intent to resell them.

No precise figures are available on the number of Canadians and U.S. citizens who go to Mexico to buy low-cost medicines, but health workers say the practice is widespread.

PRIVATE HOSPITALS AND CLINICS

Many fine private hospitals and clinics are found in the country's cities and larger towns that cater to the foreign community and wealthy Mexicans. Services provided are the same as those offered by the public facilities, but doctors often speak English and attend their patients more quickly.

Most are equipped to handle practically any emergency on a 24-hour basis and include their own pharmacy and laboratory. Another advantage of the private hospital or clinic is the possibility of requesting a particular doctor — a privilege that doesn't usually exist in public medical centers.

As in many parts of Latin America, Mexican doctors are required to work part-time in a public facility, but may operate a private practice on the side. A consultation and examination at any of the private hospitals and clinics usually run around $35.00. Prices may vary depending on the required procedures.

SERVICES PROVIDED BY PRIVATE HOSPITALS AND CLINICS INCLUDE:

- Family practice
- Cosmetic surgery
- Major dental work
- Gynecology-obstetrics
- Internal medicine
- Ophthalmology
- Orthopedics
- Pediatrics
- Full-service hospitalization
- Maternity ward
- Complete laboratory analysis
- X-ray, ultrasound and mammogram
- Intensive care coronary unit
- Electrocardiagram
- Traditional major/minor surgery
- Laparscopic surgery
- Diabetic clinic
- Holter monitoring, 24-hours
- C.A.T scanning
- Arthroscopic surgery
- Stress tests
- Clinical nutritionist
- Immunization and vaccination
- Ambulance service

DENTAL CARE

Dentists in Mexico often speak English and offer excellent basic and cosmetic procedures at prices about one-third lower than in the U.S. Most dentists charge $20.00 for the initial exam, not including any necessary X-rays. Many people, in fact, travel to Mexico solely to take advantage of low-cost, high-quality dental care. Average prices for popular treatments are as follows:

Cleaning of teeth	$25.00
Cavity fill per tooth	$25.00
Single root canal	$105.00
Tooth extraction	$28.00
Porcelain laminate per tooth	$120.00
Wisdom tooth surgery	$140.00
Removable chrome nickel bridge	$235.00

Prices vary greatly between dental offices in working-class neighborhoods and those whose clientele are foreign residents or wealthy Mexicans. Some only accept payment in U.S. dollars, but that, in no way, is an indication of their quality or capacity. Plenty of capable dentists charge in pesos and provide excellent services. Ask around.

INSURANCE

Foreigners may purchase the country's low-cost, extensive "IMSS" medical insurance or "social security." This is especially vital for expatriates, since Medicare is usually not valid outside the U.S., and most North American policies don't cover health expenses incurred abroad.

However, programs such as Blue Cross, Blue Shield, CIGNA, Travelers and few others are valid in Mexico. It's a good idea to check with your insurance company before you come down, to make sure you'll be covered.

In large cities, many private hospitals will assist expatriates in processing their claims filed to U.S. companies.

SOCIALIZED MEDICINE

The Mexican Social Security Institute (Instituto Mexicano de Seguro Social, or IMSS) charges a yearly fee of $290. Members in need of medical services can never be turned away, and become members for life, as long as their fee is current. Paid members are entitled to check-ups, all medications, lab tests, visits to a specialist, hospital stays, eye examinations, dental care and emergency ambulance service. The IMSS member pays no deductible or co-payments.

Coverage is available to the head of household and his or her dependents for the same, $290 annual premium, regardless of the number of insured family members.

Apply any time at the IMSS office nearest your home and expect to wait up to six months for final approval.

New applicants must fill out a medical questionnaire. Preexisting conditions will not be covered. The IMSS may require a medical exam at its discretion.

IMSS insurance can be a valuable safety net, especially in case of catastrophic illness and no insurance back home.

THE FINAL WORD

Most expatriates maintain their insurance coverage back home, but switch to a higher deductible. This gives them the option of returning to the U.S. for delicate surgeries or treatment of serious conditions. They rely on their IMSS coverage for routine medical care in Mexico.

Most U.S. insurance policies don't cover health expenses incurred abroad. Be sure you check with your agent before you move. The following list will help put you in touch with international insurance providers:

Travel Med	1-800-732-5309 or (301) 296-5225
Health Care Abroad	1-800-237-6615 or (703) 281-9500
Travel Assistance Int'l	1-800-821-2828 or (202) 331-1609
Access America	1-800-284-8300 or (212) 490-5345
World Care Travel Assist.	1-800-253-1877 or (213) 749-1358
Care Free Travel Insurance	1-800-645-2424 or (516) 294-0220
International SOS	1-800-523-8930 or (215) 244-1500

Ask your provider about emergency evacuation service to a U.S. hospital for urgent or delicate medical attention. Some companies provide air-ambulance service with on-board doctors and nurses, trip coordinators and global communications capabilities. Many also arrange stretcher transportation on commercial airlines. A few of these providers are:

National Jets	1-800-327-3710
North American Air Ambulance	1-800-322-8167
International SOS	1-800-523-8930
Air Ambulance Network	1-800-387-1966
Air Ambulance Int'l	1-800-227-9996
Life Flight	1-800-231-4357

USEFUL HEALTH TERMS

Call an ambulance! ¡Llame a un ambulancia!
Somebody help! ¡Socorro!

doctor:	doctor (doc-TOR)
nurse:	enfermera (en-fare-MARE-ah)
paramedic:	paramédico (para-MED-ee-coe)

First Aid:	Primeros auxilios (pree-MARE-ohs aux-ILL-ee-ohs)
emergency:	emergencia (eh-mer-HEN-see-ah)
heart problems:	problemas cardiacos (pro-BLAY-mas car-dee-AC-oes)
heart:	corazón (cor-ah-ZONE)
diabetic:	diabético (dee-ah-BET-tee-coe)
pregnant:	embarazada (em-bar-ah-ZAH-dah)
labor pains:	dolores de parto (doe-LOR-es day PAR-toe)
fever:	fiebre (fee-EH-bray)
pain:	dolor (doe-LORE)
aspirin:	aspirina (ahs-peer-EE-nah)
sprain:	torcedura (tor-say-DURE-ah)
break:	quebradura (kay-brah-DUU-rah)
cut:	cortada (cor-TAH-dah)
bruise:	cardenal (car-den-AHL)
abrasion:	raspadura (ras-pah-DUU-rah)
toothache:	dolor de muela (doe-LORE day moo-WAY-lah)
prescription:	receta (ray-SET-tah)
medicine:	medicina (med-ee-SEE-nah)
X-ray:	radiografía (rahd-ee-og-rah-FEE-ah)
To lose consciousness:	Perder conocimiento (pair-DARE coe-noe-see-mee-EN-toe)

MAKING MONEY

Global Economy -- A world-wide marketplace that knows no international borders.

With the North American Free Trade Agreement (NAFTA) in effect and Mexico's new Foreign Investment Law enacted, all the necessary safeguards are in place for a U.S. or Canadian entrepreneur to operate a business in Mexico.

The new policies have created a level playing field on which small businesses can compete for the first time with their larger counterparts for what global investors are calling part of the largest, richest market in the world.

In the past, only multinational corporations could meet Mexico's rigid former joint-venture partnership or export requirements. But now, the country has proven itself a profitable place for the foreign, "mom and pop" business owners, who are looking beyond the same old business opportunities available back home.

In his book The Global Paradox, author John Naisbitt dispels the myth that globalization will bring with it the demise of the small business. On the contrary, Naisbitt writes, "The bigger and more open the world economy becomes, the more small and middle-size companies will dominate. We have moved from economies of scale to diseconomies of scale; from bigger is better to bigger is inefficient, costly, wastefully bureaucratic, inflexible and now disastrous. The smaller and speedier players will prevail on a much expanded field."

If that doesn't motivate you to start surfing the web for business ideas abroad, listen to this — Naisbitt goes on to say that in a global economy, smaller and smaller market niches will open up. One Mexican company we know discovered its niche in small refrigerators for hotel rooms, dormitory rooms and offices. That company now sells more refrigerators to the U.S. than any other company in the world.

Mexico's attractiveness for the micro entrepreneur is enthusiastically summed up by Bill Ryan, from Chicago, who is now living in Cancún operating a small export company. "In Mexico, you can have your cake and eat it too," Ryan told us. "Mexico offers proximity to the largest consumer market in the world, product and service opportunities that are five to 10 years behind the U.S., together with a perfect climate and low cost of living."

Small business owners in Mexico are praising NAFTA's borderless economy and the country's new Foreign Investment Law, which eases restrictions on foreign business and real estate ownership and loosens residency requirements. A three-year review of NAFTA by the American Chamber of Commerce of Mexico shows that the agreement has been successful in achieving its two, primary goals: 1) to increase trade and 2) to facilitate the flow of goods and services across the borders of its member countries — Mexico, the U.S. and Canada.

Of the 1,100 people surveyed, 27 percent said they exported to the U.S. prior to NAFTA. That number jumped to 42 percent when the agreement took effect in January 1994. Prior to NAFTA, 62 percent said they imported goods from the U.S. Now, more than 76 percent do. In terms of services, more than 53 percent said NAFTA has enabled them to establish new formal business relationships with U.S. companies. The majority of these relationships are in the form of distribution agreements born of the export/import boom.

The survey proves that NAFTA has been a boon not only to large multinationals, but also to small companies, which were previously excluded from the global marketplace.

FOREIGN INVESTMENT LAW

The *new* Mexican Law of Foreign Investment (Ley de Inversión Extranjera) went into effect Dec. 28, 1993, opening the economy to foreign capital and affording national treatment to foreign investors. Unless specifically restricted by law, foreign investment is generally unlimited and doesn't require prior approval by the Mexican government. While the investment law and NAFTA are complementary, in the case of conflict or discrepancy, NAFTA will be given preference under Mexican law. See the appendix for an English translation of this law and for foreign investment restrictions.

NAFTA

NAFTA's main goal is to ensure long-term trade cooperation between the U.S., Canada and Mexico. NAFTA negotiations concluded in August 1992. The agreement took effect Jan. 1, 1994. The agreement phased-out all tariffs and other barriers to trade, services and investment among its three partners over a 15-year period.

One of the most significant features of the agreement opens Mexico's $150 billion services market to U.S. and Canadian banks, telecommunications companies, insurance and accounting firms, trucking companies and other businesses. NAFTA has also improved access to Canada's $300 billion services market.

NAFTA is especially important to the business owner because it locks-in Mexican economic and market reforms and ensures basic policy will not change resulting from short-term difficulties. Without the agreement, investor confidence would fall substantially.

As Mexico is forced to open more sectors of its economy to foreign competition, NAFTA is expected to have a negative short-term effect on the economy, including the displacement of thousands of workers and the expansion of poverty. But the agreement's long-term rewards of sustainable development will convert the country into one of the world's largest and richest market places.

BENEFITS TO SMALL BUSINESSES

NAFTA eliminates numerous tariff and non-tariff barriers among Mexico, Canada and the U.S. on each country's imports and exports to each other. The agreement provides increased market access for small business. The elimination and simplification of numerous procedures, from customs regulations to quality standards, enable small businesses to take advantage of the Mexican market as never before.

By lowering costs and dissolving barriers, NAFTA will help smaller businesses penetrate the Mexican market without having to invest in Mexico.

Further information about NAFTA provisions and the status of congressional approval by the three partners can be obtained from the U.S. Department of Commerce Flash Facts Hotline, at (202) 482-4464. See the appendix for more on how NAFTA can benefit the small business owner.

WHO ARE THE CONSUMERS?

Approximately 80 percent of Mexico's 93 million people are under the age of 40, and 50 percent are under the age of 25. The birth rate has fallen from 3.3 percent to 2 percent since 1980. Nearly 70 percent of the population lives in urban areas, specifically Mexico City (20 million), Guadalajara (4 million), Monterrey (2.9 million), Puebla (1.5 million), León (1.2 million) and in some 70 other cities with populations ranging from 100,000 to 900,000.

One-third of the population works in some 1.3 million establishments, 97 percent of which are considered "micro," small and medium sized. A large firm employs 500 or more workers.

Two percent of Mexico's population is considered upper-class, characterized by a high level of education, luxury housing, multiple vehicles and international travel. About 20 percent of the population is considered upper-middle class, comprising mostly university-educated professionals, who own their homes, have at least one vehicle, buy a wide range of household appliances and occasionally travel outside Mexico. About 49 percent of Mexicans are members of the lower-middle class, living in smaller homes and spending a greater percentage of their income on basic necessities. The rural, under-employed and unemployed workers do the best they can.

About 60 percent of Mexican households have an annual income of less than $8,000. Nearly 24 percent have an annual income of between $8,000 and $24,000. Nine percent earn between $26,000 and $58,000 yearly, and 6 percent bring home more than $60,000 annually.

Upper Class The leading salary earner in an upper-class Mexican household tends to be a top executive, company owner or non-managerial professional, such as lawyer or doctor. They tend to shop for groceries at supermarkets and specialty shops and buy clothing and durable goods at department stores or boutiques. They shop for the latest fashions and electronics when traveling abroad.

Middle Class The middle class salary earner tends to be an employed professional, civil servant, entrepreneur or small businessperson. This group usually shops for groceries at supermarkets, convenience stores and wholesales and for clothing and durable goods in self-service stores, small shopping centers and urban commercial areas.

Lower Class Lower class wage earners usually work in blue-collar jobs, such as shopkeeper, mechanic, office assistant or secretary. They tend to buy food items and clothing as needed in convenience stores and public markets or from street vendors.

Major marketing areas include:

Central Area Around Mexico City, this area is home to 20 million consumers. The area includes Puebla, Toluca, Cuernavaca and Pachuca. This is the political, commercial, financial and cultural center of the country.

Bajio Area This population center of 6 million people is anchored by the city of Guadalajara and includes the surrounding communities of León, Aguascalientes, Celaya and Irapuato. This is an important commerical, industrial and agricultural area.

Northern Area The Northern city of Monterrey serves as the hub for this region of 4.7 million consumers that includes the surrounding cities of Torreón, Saltillo and Monclovia. The region is an important industrial center, producing steel, glass, textiles, beverages, paper, chemicals and other products.

U.S./Mexico Border This 2,000-mile region is home to more than 3 million inhabitants in the towns of Juárez, Tijuana, Mexicali, Matamoros, Reynosa and Nuevo Laredo. This is an active industrial, agricultural and tourist area. Mexican firms manufacture a variety of products that offer excellent opportunities for export sales of machinery, equipment, industrial raw materials, replacement parts, accessories, service, know-how and direct sales to major international companies, such as the automotive assembly industry.

WHY MEXICO?

Many North American entrepreneurs are unaware of the enormous growth potential that exists right in their own back yard. The U.S. has only 10 percent of the world's population. Only half of U.S. products are sold overseas, and only one-third of foreign products are sold in the U.S. Many North American-based companies are already making more money from opportunities abroad than from those at home. In fact, 75 percent of all growth in world trade will take place in developing countries. Who will be the big benefactors of this growth? Small and mid-sized companies, that's who. Here's what Mexico and the region has to offer:

❧Consumer markets in Latin America will exceed those of Europe and Japan by 2010.

❧Mexico's emerging middle class is opening up and demanding consumer goods as never before.

❧The region shares a generally "pro-U.S." attitude.

❧Political and commercial risk is considerably less than in Asia, Eastern Europe or the former Soviet Union.

❧Europe and Asia can't compete with Mexico's inexpensive labor costs.

❧High quality labor force.

❂NAFTA

❂Mexico's other regional trade agreements further facilitate
  doing business.

LOCATION

U.S. companies have traditionally enjoyed two main advantages when doing business in Mexico: 1) a large domestic market
potential and 2) a competitive base for plant operations. What
we'd like to add to the list is one very important consideration:
location.

Mexico's proximity to the U.S. and its desire to go global
creates the following benefits:

❂The country's new openness provides ample opportunities
  for both sales and investment in a developing market located close to home.

❂Mexico serves as the doorway to the rest of Latin America,
  providing a pool of professionals fluent in the language and
  familiar with Latin culture.

❂U.S. and Canadian companies can take advantage of well-
  established Mexican manufacturing, marketing and distribution channels to improve efficiency.

❂Mexico's business and consumer groups have developed a
  strong familiarity with U.S. consumer lifestyles and business culture.

❂Mexico has trade agreements with many Central and South
  American countries, providing open access to Mexico-based
  U.S. and Canadian firms.

SMALL BUSINESS OPTIONS

Still undecided about which business is best for you in Mexico?
Business opportunities fall within two, main categories: import-

ing products to Mexico, and making a direct investment in the Mexican economy through manufacturing, tourism, service or exporting. The following list may help narrow the possibilities:

IMPORTING TO MEXICO

Introducing a new product to Mexico is perhaps the first opportunity most entrepreneurs encounter when considering doing business south-of-the-border. This is because they may be already using, manufacturing or selling a product domestically that they feel has potential in Mexico.

A product that sells well in the U.S. should also be well accepted in Mexico, but be sure to take the necessary steps and analyze all the possibilities.

Because of the former, restrictive government policies that placed prohibitive tariffs and regulations on U.S. products, Mexican consumers are maybe 10 years behind on certain products that people in the U.S. take for granted.

Depending on your desire to establish an office in-country, you can export to Mexico under one of the following schemes:

DIRECT SALES

Direct sales to a Mexican customer are usually done with unique products that have a limited number of potential buyers. Their clients are easy to identify and contact. Many times the U.S. business owner will contract an agent to distribute the product throughout Mexico.

CONTRACTING A DISTRIBUTOR

Business owners new to Mexico often hire a local representative to ensure the timely and accurate placement of the product in the national market. The agent is subject to the Federal Labor Law in Mexico, so be sure to have your attorney design a contract that is beneficial to you.

LICENSING AGREEMENT

Licensing agreements are relatively new to Mexico, since the government removed restrictions on them in 1990. Licensing involves making your experience or technical skills available — for a price. Licensing offers a rapid entry into the market at a low initial investment by allowing a Mexican company to manufacture and sell your product in return for payment.

JOINT VENTURE

Joint ventures are also an easy way to enter the market without substantial capital outlay. In a joint venture, a U.S. company brings the expertise and equipment, while the Mexican company supplies the market knowledge, inexpensive labor and most suitable method of distribution. A joint venture with a well-established Mexican company brings a lot of marketing and strategic benefits.

CUSTOMS REQUIREMENTS

In 1989 the Mexican government enacted customs reforms that cut much of the red tape and simplified what was once bureaucratic and unorganized. All the problems haven't disappeared, but at least the government is renewing its efforts to modernize and respond to common complaints by U.S. exporters.

Only a Mexican corporation or resident of Mexico can import goods into the country. In addition, you must be registered with the Secretary of Finance and Public Credit (*Secretaría de Hacienda y Crédito Público, Hacienda*); have a federal taxpayer number (*Registro Federal de Contribuyentes, RFC*); be registered in the National Importers Registry (*Padrón de Importadores*); and be registered with the appropriate industrial-sector import registry, in limited cases.

NAFTA has eliminated most of its license and permit requirements on goods imported from the U.S., but some still apply. Currently, only 148 of the approximately 10,000 imported products require an import license.

CUSTOMS DUTIES

All import documents must be prepared and submitted by a licensed Mexican customs broker.

Imports not qualifying for NAFTA's tariff-free status are subject to an ad-valorem duty (AVD), usually 20 percent assessed on the cost or more, depending on the goods, insurance and freight value of the shipment. All tariffs will be phased out over the next 15 years, depending on the type of goods. Also, a 15 percent value-added tax is assessed on the total value of the goods and their respective duties.

NAFTA has eliminated much of the red-tape in transporting merchandise across the border, but the system is still far from efficient. The agreement stipulates that U.S. truckers will have nationwide access to Mexico on Jan. 1, 2000. Until then, U.S. trucking companies cannot bring merchandise directly into Mexico from the U.S. At the border, the U.S. company transfers its trailer to the rig of a Mexican company with which it shares a business relationship.

Be sure to hire a transportation company that offers a basic insurance plan to cover damage or loss. As a rule of thumb, it's best to insure the merchandise for the total value plus 10 to 20 percent. Research the customer service history of the company. Talk to previous customers if possible. A little homework before you contract can save a big headache later on.

FINDING A MARKET

The best way to introduce your product to Mexico, as well as meet important distributors and customs brokers, is to attend a Mexican trade show. In 1990, there were very few exhibitions in Mexico, but by 1996 more than 250 shows and 70 municipal fairs were staged throughout the country.

DIRECT INVESTMENT

The Mexican domestic goods and services industry needs you! Come for a few extended visits and determine what you can provide that people -- foreign and national -- will pay for, whether it be a mail service, messenger service, catering service, quality carpentry, crafts, consulting, tour operating, whatever. Then come on down and do it better than anyone else.

MANUFACTURING

An abundant and inexpensive labor pool and logistically desirable location have made Mexico among the most sought-after places in the world for many types of assembly work and production. The recent devaluation of the peso should keep labor costs low, at least in the short run, and provide stiff competition for other nations with a strong maquila industry, such as Asia.

Mexican manufacturing generally ranges from small to medium-size companies. Of the approximately 123,000 companies currently operating here, 98 percent are micro, small or mid-size businesses — all with fewer than 250 employees.

The manufacturing industry is Mexico's biggest income-generator. Almost all materials used to manufacture chemical products, electrical and electronic components, textiles and footwear come from the United States. Less than 2 percent of these materials come from Mexico.

THE MAQUILA INDUSTRY

The "maquiladora" manufacturing program allows foreign companies to set up factories in Mexico where they can import capital goods, machinery, raw materials, parts and components used for exports on a temporary, duty-free basis. The maquiladora industry in Mexico has grown steadily and now boasts more than 2,400 plants that employ nearly 600,000 workers.

The greatest strength of Mexico's maquiladora plants lies in their competitive labor force, their proximity to the world's largest markets and the country's own growing market. As of 1994, maquiladoras are allowed to sell up to 55 percent of the previous year's exports within Mexico. Among NAFTA countries, this percentage increases by 5 percent annually until the limit of sales to the domestic market is lifted entirely in the year 2001. These benefits have caused plants in Central American and the Caribbean to flee to Mexico in search of higher profits.

Until the year 2000, the maquiladora industry will be for the most part unaffected. The only substantial change will be the gradually increasing amount that a plant may sell in the domestic market. From 2001 on, the maquila industry will change dramatically as it is absorbed into the national manufacturing base and is able to sell all its goods in the Mexican marketplace.

TOURISM

Tourism and travel is the world's largest industry. Mexico is the world's eighth most popular tourist destination and holds thirteenth place for income produced.

Each year, more than 16 million visitors inject more than $5 billion into the Mexican economy. Next to manufacturing and petroleum, tourism is the country's largest earner of foreign currency. Mexico's tourism industry has experienced the fastest growth among all sectors of the economy in the last five years.

As a result of the aggressive economic liberalization during the Salinas administration, foreign direct investment in Mexico over the past five years has nearly doubled the total foreign investment of all previous years combined.

The Foreign Investment Law of 1993 liberalized Mexico's policy regulating all aspects of foreign investment. The law created significant new opportunities for foreign investment in tourism-related activities.

The kiosk, located in the central park of many Mexican cities and towns, is a popular place to gather and socialize.

It is now possible for international investors to retain 100 percent ownership in industries such as travel agencies, cruise ship lines, restaurants and nightclubs. Foreign investors may also own up to 49 percent of marinas and 25 percent of the equity in domestic and specialized air transportation businesses.

Foreign investors may purchase land anywhere in the country without government approval, including within the so-called "restricted areas" 31 miles from any coastline or 62 miles from any border, as long as the land will not be used for residential purposes.

Private citizens may acquire residential property in the restricted zones through a trust, which allows foreigners to hold title for renewable periods of 50 years.

Opportunities in the transportation sector have also become available through the "frequency liberty" policies, which now permit foreign airlines to fly at full capacity to destinations in Mexico not previously authorized by the government. Authorization procedures for charter flights have also been liberalized and simplified.

DESTINATIONS

Most tourists end up at one of Mexico's beautiful beach areas, but as more and more discover the interior colonial cities, inland opportunities have surged.

Located far from foreign influence and English-speaking tour guides, colonial cities offer something most beach resorts don't — the culture of the real Mexico. Business opportunities include bed and breakfasts, Spanish schools, restaurants and small export companies that distribute handicrafts and other unique goods found in these regions. The following colonial cities offer exceptional opportunity for the innovative entrepreneur:

Zacatecas Surrounded by the mountains of central Mexico, this colonial mining town is the capital of the state of Zacatecas, noted for its rich architecture and the famous Cerro de la Bufa.

Puebla Southeast of Mexico City, Puebla's colonial art dif-

fers from the rest of the country. Its colonial houses were decorated with tiles, and their expansive orange-tree-filled gardens were
enclosed with art-adorned fences. Popular attractions include the
Templo de la Compañía, La Casa del Dean, La Casa de los
Muñecos and the Cathedral.

San Miguel de Allende Located in the state of Guanajuato,
northwest of Mexico City, this town is surrounded by mountain
ranges and has steep, zigzagging streets. San Miguel is popular
with both Mexican and foreign tourists as an important artisan
center where sarapes, shawls, paper maché objects, ceramics
and pewter are produced. Major attractions include the huge,
neogothic Iglesia Parroquial, the Plaza de Allende, Casa del
Conde and Casa Loja.

Cholula Home to archaeological ruins that are considered
the most important proof of old-world Mexico, Cholula is within
easy driving distance of Puebla. Ruins of pyramids remain under
temples like the Santuario de los Remedios, which is one of the
365 churches said to have existed here.

Guadalajara Capital of the state of Jalisco, Guadalajara's
mariachis, jarabe tapatío and tequila have come to represent the
entire country. Full of natural beauty, history, art and a wide variety of handicrafts, this city is especially popular with retired foreigners. Places of interest include Centro Histórico, Parque Mirador
Independencia, Tonala, Ciudad Tequila, Chapala, Ajijic and more.

Guanajuato This city, in south-central Mexico, is rich in
history and art, with multiple baroque buildings and French-
style palaces from the era of former President Porfirio Díaz.
The city is famous for its Festival Cervantino and the traditional street singing performed by students sporting colonial
dress. Main attractions include Teatro Juárez, Callejón del Beso,
Mercado Hidalgo, Alhondiga de Granaditas, Museo de las
Momias and more.

Patzcuaro West of Mexico City, this town features steep
cobblestone streets and is bordered by Patzcuaro Lake, with its
many "islands of Janitzio." Many handicrafts are produced and
sold here. Places to visit include the Casa de los Once Patios,
Museo de Artes Populares and the lake islands.

Morelia The cultural treasures of this city, west of the capital, are personified in its magnificent baroque cathedral with neoclassic interior. Other points of interest include the Templo de San Augustín, San Francisco and the Colegio de San Nicolás.

Taxco Filled with quaint, quiet neighborhoods and fascinating cobblestone streets, Taxco is located southwest of Mexico City. The town is famous for its red-tiled roofs and silver artisan workshops.

COASTAL RESORTS

Mexico is renown for its first-class Riviera, and Cancún, on the eastern tip of the Yucatán Peninsula, is one of the world's premier tourist destinations with two million visitors per year. The Pacific resort town of Ixtapa, located 150 miles north of Acapulco, is second only to Cancún in terms of tourism revenue generated. The following is a list of the country's premier resort towns:

Acapulco An international meeting place and a port of unequaled beauty, Acapulco is located on Mexico's South Pacific coast. Its mountainous landscape covered with tropical vegetation cascades down to a beautiful bay. Its tropical climate makes it one of the most visited summer ports. Popular places to visit include Isla Roqueta, La Quebrada, Laguna de Coyuca, Pie de la Cuesta and Papagayo National Park.

Cabo San Lucas Located on the tip of the Baja California Peninsula, Cabo San Lucas is famous for its world-class sport fishing and beautiful beaches.

Cancún Known world-over for its modern and functional architecture, multiple water sports, white-sand beaches, emerald-green waters and sweltering sun, Cancún offers an incomparable mix of beauty, entertainment and convenience for the international traveler.

Bahías de Huatulco Home to a group of bays with crystal-clear waters, where the fine sand contrasts with rocky coastal terrain, Bahías de Huatulco is one of the country's newest tourist destinations. Places to visit in this South Pacific paradise include Bahía de Santa Cruz and Bahía Chahue.

Ixtapa - Zihuatanejo Only 125 miles northwest of Acapulco, this community is on a bay surrounded by mountains and enjoys a cozy atmosphere. Main attractions include Playa Madera, La Ropa and Las Gatas.

Loreto This was the site of the first settlement on Baja California in 1697 and still preserves its traditional essence today. It's coastal beauty is enhanced by the convenience of other popular beaches, including nearby Napolo Beach.

Manzanillo This town's modern port and infrastructure doesn't detract from its beautiful beaches. Some of the tourists' favorite spots include Playa Audiencia, Playa Santiago and the Cuyutlan Lake.

Mazatlán A popular Pacific destination for cruise ships, Mazatlán is known for its beautiful sunsets, many islands, rocks and beaches. Aside from ample tourism services, the town is home to many recreational activities, including world-class marlin and sailfish tournaments and the famous carnival. Main attractions include the Sábalo, Gaviotas and Cerritos beaches, Isla Venados, Isla Pájaros and the Shell Museum.

Puerto Vallarta Located on the Pacific side near the mouth of the Sea of Cortés, this famous tourist center features rustic cobblestone streets and houses with red-tile roofs that contrast culturally with the beach resort hotels. Best places include Playa Guayabitos, Mismaloya, Boca de Tomatlan and Yelapa.

Puerto Escondido and Puerto Angel Both small bays off the coast of Oaxaca in Southern Mexico, these communities feature tranquil beaches bordered by gentle slopes thick with vegetation.

Veracruz This warm city on the Gulf of Mexico was the country's first trading and sailing port. Once a year, the famous carnival brings the sleepy town alive with music, dancing and color. Places of interest include the picturesque downtown area, the San Juan de Ulua Fort and Punta Antón Lizardo.

Oxaca This southern coastal region is among Mexico's most colorful. It's a favorite with expat residents and tourists alike.

SMALL BUSINESS START UPS

O ne of the biggest myths of doing business in Mexico is the difficulty North American small-business owners have setting up a commercial activity. Laws easing foreign business ownership have been in effect for four years now, but you'll still encounter a plethora of armchair business consultants and even licensed Mexican attorneys who are not yet aware of all the changes. Don't listen to these people.

Foreigners may own businesses in Mexico as sole proprietors (*empresa de persona física*) or as independent legal entities, such as a corporation (sociedad anónima), partnership or as a branch of a foreign company. The type of "presence" you want to establish in Mexico is a big consideration in the formation of your company.

Most North Americans own businesses in Mexico as sole proprietors under a FM-3 or FM-2 visa status (see Residency chapter for more info). If you want to operate as a sole proprietor you must first obtain the FM-3 or 2 resident visa under the classification "Visitor Remunerated." Without this status, the business must be set up as an independent legal entity. The FM-3 and 2 are less expensive to obtain than a legal entity, and owning a business as a sole proprietor offers certain tax advantages. For example, sole proprietors pay taxes on their net income, not the 35 percent of gross income required of corporations.

The residency visa is also required to establish a corporation, if you're planning on living year-round in Mexico. Corporations offer certain asset protection advantages that you may find preferable. Always discuss your business plans with a reputable attorney before plunging ahead.

BUSINESS ENTITIES

Business entities include: corporations, partnerships, joint ventures, branch offices and licensing agreements. You may also register as an agent or distributor. Like in the U.S. and Canada, each entity offers a distinct set of advantages.

The **corporation with variable capital** (SA de CV) is the most frequently established business entity. It must have a minimum fixed capital of $50,000 pesos. With the **limited liability partnership** (sociedad de responsabilidad limitada S de RL), the minimum required start-up capital is only $3,000 pesos. Investors are only liable for the amount of their own contributions to that capital. The **branch of a foreign corporation** (sucursal de sociedad extranjera) classification applies to a foreign company that opens a branch office in Mexico. The cost to set up a foreign corporation in Mexico runs between $800 and $5,000, depending on the complexity.

GETTING STARTED

Don't expect much assistance from organizations that claim to help North American business owners in Mexico. Organizations like the American Chamber of Commerce or the U.S. Embassy mostly cater to the multinational corporation, not the micro-entrepreneur.

However, it is still a good idea to stop in and meet with their representatives, hang out in their resource libraries and generally pick the brains of the people who are there. The following three organizations are good starting points. Canadians should consult with their embassy for equivalents:

The American Chamber of Commerce of Mexico is your best starting place. Their main office is in Mexico City, but it also has branch offices in Guadalajara and Monterrey. The Chamber works with other organizations promoting Mexico-U.S. trade and acts as an information clearinghouse. It is a prime source for developing valuable business contacts. The Chamber has some 2,900 corporate members in Mexico.

The U.S. Commercial Service Department is also a good place to mingle, as you peruse its libraries and talk with its representatives. It offers numerous programs to help large companies hook up with potential clients and find investment information. Every branch of the U.S. Embassy in Mexico has one of these offices.

U.S. State Offices in Mexico serve as extensions of each state's Department of Commerce. Their sole function is to promote the expansion of trade with Mexico. They're privy to a wealth of information about markets, distribution and possible representatives or clients. See our resource section for their many locations in Mexico.

TIPS FOR SMALL BUSINESS OWNERS

Many products and services are still needed in Mexico. The following tips should help you determine how to successfully find a niche and provide what the market is lacking. Remember: the key to any successful venture is research.

Follow the money Tourism is a leading source of Mexico's foreign revenue. Visit the gift shops, English-language bookstores, hotels and street vendors. Take as many tours as you can and visit tourist-related businesses to see if there is anything that you can provide better. Filling a market need is the best way to get your foot in the door.

Don't forget the locals Mexico has a wealthy upper class and a growing middle class that don't mind spending a little extra on products and services that meet their needs and exceptions. Imported cosmetics and U.S.-quality clothing, as well as certain tools, toys, kitchen supplies, building products and electronics are highly sought after, but hard to find in Mexico. Talk to the locals; they'll give you plenty of good ideas.

Expatriate market More than 500,000 full-time foreign residents live in Mexico at least six months out of the year. Hang around the American Legion, Democrats or Republicans Abroad, the Rotary Club or other popular clubs and organizations to find out what local expatriates are longing for.

New technology Mexico now offers many of the latest computer and techno gadgets that can be found in North America. But a niche still exists for those that can provide the very newest of gadgets before the others catch on. Maybe you could do it.

Look to the countryside The Mexican countryside is filled with obscure artisans who have been mastering their craft for years. You would be surprised at the quality of locally made products that can be found in and around Guanajuato, Chiapas or Oaxaca. The proper U.S. contacts could make for a thriving export business that could even supply local tourist markets.

CAN I GET RICH?

Entrepreneurs all over the world have been asking themselves since the dawn of time, "Will I get rich from this?" Keep in mind that a highly successful business in Mexico may not take in as much as a mediocre counterpart up north. That's where lower cost-of-living comes into play. Mexico's cheap lifestyles and low business start-up costs will save you a bundle.

For many, profits don't matter much. The romance of owning an import/export business or small hotel in a far-a-way place is a lifestyle they just wouldn't pass up. But enough opportunity exists in Mexico to, at the very least, provide you with a steady income on which you can live comfortably or supplement your retirement benefits.

THE MIRACLE OF COMPOUNDED SAVINGS

Compound interest is the interest that accrues on both the principal and the past unpaid accrued interest. Compound interest is earned on both the principal and on the interest accumulated over the preceding periods.

Say you own two taco carts in a prime tourist area of Puerto Vallarta. Each cart nets you $1,200 per month after taxes for a total of $2,400. Since your low monthly living expenses in Mexico total only $1,000, you can save $1,400 per month or $16,800 per year (Refer to the chart).

After spending a few thousand dollars on a trip or on some new clothes, you invest, say, $10,000 in a U.S. mutual-fund or maybe an investment account in an offshore Caribbean bank. Your investment fund averages a 12.6 percent return. Compound this annually, and invest $10,000 every year for 20 years. In 20 years' time, the profits from your taco carts will have accumulated to over $990,760. Not bad!

Lifestyle makes these kind of savings possible in Mexico. Where in the U.S. or Canada could you live on $1,000 per month?

Here's another example. Say you moved to Guadalajara and started a small typing and translation service. You hire two bilingual employees from the local university to handle your clients. They earn $300 per month — a pretty good salary for a couple of college students in Mexico.

You spend your time administering the company and marketing your services. After paying all office expenses and your personal living expenses, you are able to save around $400 per month, or $5,000 a year. You're 40 years old and plan to buy a house by the time your 50. If you put away $5,000 every year into a mutual-fund for 10 years, earning a 12.6 percent return, compounded annually, you'll end up saving $120,000 — enough to buy a nice house in Mexico. During that same 10-year period, you could expand your office or add other locations to make even more money.

THE ROAD TO RICHES

20 Years to Retirement			10 Years to Retirement		
Present Savings*	Annual Contributions	20-Year Accummulation	Present Savings*	Annual Contributions	10-Year Accummulation
NONE	$2,000	$198,152	NONE	$2,000	$48,063
NONE	5,000	495,380	NONE	5,000	120,157
NONE	10,000	990,760	NONE	10,000	241,313
NONE	20,000	1,981,520	NONE	20,000	480,626

*Assumes 12.6 percent annual return, compounding in a regular U.S. or Caribbean brokerage or mutual fund account.

We did leave out two "monkey wrenches" that will reduce your earnings somewhat: taxes and inflation.

Always consult with an investment advisor about the best ways to place your money in a tax-deferred retirement account. Many people decide to invest "offshore" in accounts that are "tax free." The Caribbean is brimming with these types of accounts, going at high interest rates, but that doesn't mean its tax free. Don't walk the thin line between tax evasion and tax avoidance without consulting with an expert or conducting thorough research. Your life savings are at stake.

When it comes to building wealth, the magic of compounding interest makes the need to invest a lot of money unnecessary. Don't let the lengthy time periods discourage you. If you'd started this 10 years ago, today you'd be going to the bank to collect your money!

STILL WONDERING IF YOU COULD GET RICH?

In a June 1997 article in Money magazine titled "7 Secrets to Achieve Your Money Dreams," author Tony Cook described how the regular guy could become rich in the U.S. He developed his seven rules based on the best-selling new book, *The Millionaire Next Door*, by Thomas J. Stanley and William D. Danko.

Cook says that the keys to achieving millionaire status are extreme thriftiness; disciplined, prodigious investing; an aversion to debt; serious tax sheltering; help from at least one sharp financial advisor and hard work, ideally at your own business.

If these qualities lead to wealth in industrialized nations, imagine what you could do with them in Mexico! The following is our adaptation for Mexico of Cook's seven golden rules. Take them to heart, and you'll be on your way to your first million.

1. Live below your means It costs at least half as much to live in Mexico as it does farther north. To maintain the lifestyle that $1,000 per month can buy a couple in Mexico, you'd have to earn at least $3,000 farther north — and you still won't have a full-time housekeeper.

2. **Budget your spending meticulously** Keep track of every peso you spend. Just because everything is cheap, don't spend money on things you don't need. Make a belt-tight budget and stick to it.

3. **Launch a disciplined savings and investment plan** Most millionaires sock away at least 15 percent of their income before taxes, and many put aside 20 percent or more. Even if you earn just $2,000 a month in Mexico, you should be able to save 50 percent or $1,000 per month. That's $12,000 a year or more than $250,000 in just 10 years, at 12.6 percent compounded annually!

4. **Take on debt sparingly** Most expats don't use credit cards or get bank loans. Many reevaluate their needs and discover that their wants in Mexico are much simpler. The country's low cost-of-living makes credit cards unnecessary, and ultra high interest rates make bank loans unfeasible.

5. **Hire a astute, independent financial advisor** Find an expert you can trust who will give you his or her objective opinion about your investment plans. Be sure to keep your money in dollars; pesos are too risky.

6. **Pay as little as (legally) possible in income taxes** There are many things you can do to keep your tax burden low. A) Invest in growth stocks whose gains come mostly in price appreciation that is not taxed until the stocks are sold. B) Invest in real estate, which is not taxed until the property is sold. C) Max-out on your tax-deferred retirement account. Hire a tax accountant who knows the laws for citizens living abroad and study up on your offshore investment options. You'll find there are legal ways to invest your money offshore avoiding the high tax rates back home.

7. **Finally, start your own business** Self-employed people are four times more likely to be millionaires than people who earn a paycheck working for others. In Mexico it's probably ten times easier to start your own business than in the U.S. or Canada.

After reading about the miracles of compound interest and Tony Cook's seven rules to riches, you're probably starting to see how the business owner in Mexico, making the same amount of money as the one in the U.S., can retire with twice as much money or in half as much time.

OVERSEAS OPPORTUNITIES 2000

The savvy North American entrepreneur looking for new products and new markets can no longer ignore the abundance of opportunities in Mexico.

With the opening of borders, many Mexican companies are struggling to provide the quality of service and merchandise that North Americans have taken for granted for years.

Mexico's low cost of living, relatively low business start-up costs, and low wages are probably the entrepreneur's greatest incentive to operate here. A couple can live modestly on less than $1,000 per month and still have enough left over for such luxuries as a housekeeper, gardener and dining out. Depending on the type of business, start-up costs — including lawyers' fees, business permits and employee salaries (averages $10.00 per day) — will probably total less than half of their U.S. or Canadian equivalents.

The small entrepreneur can take advantage of a vigorous import and export market, invest in tourism, start a small manufacturing company or provide a service to the domestic market. Opportunities in Mexico are only limited to your imagination. The country's lack of distribution infrastructure opens the door to incredible opportunities in multilevel marketing (MLM) and telemarketing. Both are relatively new business opportunities in Mexico.

Enormous profits can be made by providing a service or product that other foreigners may consider to be beneath them. Sometimes the simplest of ideas leads to a steady growth company that translates into thousands of dollars.

The following ideas are only some of the opportunities that exist in Mexico for investors of every budget, level of experience and professional background. They are not only thought provoking and inspirational, but legitimate businesses that you can start right now. Business classifications are based on minimum start-up capital: $3,000 or less, $10,000 or less and more than $10,000. So what do you think? Got any good ideas?

START-UPS FOR LESS THAN $3,000

Souvenirs and handicraft sales Just about everyone visiting Mexico brings home a broad-brimmed sombrero, paper maché parrot, tee shirt or ethnic handicraft. Souvenir sales through tourism tap into the buying power of Mexico's 16 million yearly visitors.

Visit colonial towns and seek out artisans to become your "work force." Try to come up with original ideas and then let your artisans inject their own creative juices to design and manufacture unique gifts that you can sell to local gift shops in airports, hotels and tourist centers, or export to gift shops abroad.

The keys to success in this business are creativity and innovation. Offer gifts that deviate from the norm; gifts that will call to shoppers from the shop shelves. Don't think there's no room for innovation in this business. In El Salvador, an environmentally conscious entrepreneur recognized the value of a new paper manufactured from discarded banana husks rather than trees. Today, he and his partners manufacture rustic notepads, agendas, drawing pads and stationary sets featuring "banana paper." They now export to neighboring Costa Rica, Nicaragua and Honduras, as well as the U.S.

Publishing Mexico is home to many, successful, "first-time" publishers. One enterprising young woman in Cancún came up with the idea to publish a business directory in this popular resort town. She charges the business around $30 for a line-listing and more for a display add. It's a publisher's dream to have advertisements on every page, and her Cancún Business Directory has more then 10 ad's per page! Advertising revenue pays for the printing and puts a nice profit in her pocket, plus she sells her directory in stores to make even more money. She's now considering branching out to other Mexican cities.

The keys, again, are creativity and innovation. For example, why not publish a children's coloring book, where all the illustrations feature local, kid-related businesses that have each "bought" a page. A real estate magazine could become a magnet for local advertisers, as could business directories, entertainment guides or tourist publications — calendars, post cards, directories of services where English is spoken, language books. With ample advertising, you can sometimes give the books away and still come out ahead.

Distribution The distribution of books, magazines, souvenirs and tee-shirts to gift shops and stores throughout Mexico would be a tough business to get going, but tremendous opportunities exist for the right person. The largest book and magazine distributor in Mexico is DIMSA, followed by a few "mom and pop" companies. Vendors could leave their products with you for distribution on consignment to local stores or shops. You could also charge consignment customers monthly, and restock the shelves, as needed — for a 15 to 30 percent commission on total sales.

Plenty of good, marketable products are out there with vendors that would love to have you distribute for them. This is a great opportunity for go-getters who will work hard to provide superior distribution and collections, reaching sales points usually not serviced by the big distributors, like bed and breakfasts and smaller souvenir shops.

Resident Application Processor Hundreds of newcomers to Mexico apply for their FM-2 and 3 resident visas every month, often paying exorbitant fees to local attorneys. But this process is something anyone can do. Mexican lawyers charge $1,000 or more for this service. You can charge half that price and still have a thriving business.

Entrepreneurs not fluent in Spanish can hire a local or two to make the Immigration runs for you. This will enable you to drum up business and concentrate on customer service. To get a edge on your competition, market your services in foreign publications or with the U.S. and Canadian consulates.

Export Clothing to the U.S., Canada and the World The apparel industry in Mexico manufactures quality, inexpensive clothing that you could buy in bulk at discount rates to resell up north. Many North American consumers love the Mexican serapes, and the colorful, traditional clothing unique to Mexico's Indian villages. With NAFTA, this type of clothing can be readily purchased and shipped across the border with relative ease. Something sure to catch-on northward are those "Don Juan or Zorro-style" white collar shirts with long sleeves. And those white sun dresses with intricate embroidery would go over big with sun worshipers abroad.

Mexico also manufactures clothing for big U.S. brands. An entrepreneur with the inside tract could buy clothing (without the label) at bulk discount rates for resale up north through your own clothing outlet or at swap meets. Sell it yourself or find distributors across the country to place your goods and help you with collections.

Public Advertising Sign Company Mexicans advertise their products and services on everything from bus stops to the sides of old buildings in small towns. You can start a business that offers small billboard advertising in restaurants and in public restrooms. Talk with taxi company cooperatives or individual cab owners to put advertising directly on their cabs.

Something new to U.S. markets that would also work in Mexico is placing small billboard advertisements in public and private schools. Be creative and find your advertisers and placement locations before you spend any money. A contract with a big national drink or clothing company here could net you some hefty profits.

Internet Consulting and World Wide Web Page Design Start a company in this new and dynamic field that targets national and international corporations. Show companies how they can save money on long-distance telephone rates by using e-mail, Internetphone and videoconferencing. Help them design and put up a "store front" on the World Wide Web. Intranet, or internal e-mail communication, is in its initial stage in Mexico. According to Grupo Pisa, less then 20 percent of the larger companies use it. Most businesses still don't use the Internet, but would like to know more.

Contact these companies to give them a personal demonstration on how you can save them time and money. Most will be trying to tap the North American market or keep in touch with their home-base abroad. Foreigners excel in this business due to their knowledge of cultures and languages abroad.

Desktop Publishing, Graphic Arts and Public Relations As Mexico continues to go global, companies of all sizes will increasingly need creative, articulate people who speak the language of the powerful North American consumer. If you're good with a jingle and have an eye for art, offer your services to small local exporters. Once you develop a loyal clientele, you'll have to hire an assistant or two to keep up with demand.

Comic Photography Business Set up a series of "stages" featuring classic, Mexican scenes that tourists can "become part of" to have their picture taken. For example, acquire a realistic, paper maché or fiberglass "charging bull" that your clients can pose with, dressed in full, bullfighter regalia.

Or set up an overstuffed chair where clients can have their picture taken with a beautiful Mexican seductress or muscle-bound Mexican hunk. Or how about a primative scene featuring the infamous Aztec stone table your clients can "become part of" with wardrobe materials you supply, to enact a traditional human sacrifice.

Tourists will pay up to $5.00 each for these farcical photos. Open a studio in a shopping mall or popular tourist center. Twenty customers a day will net you around $3,000 per month — enough to keep you laughing all the way to the bank.

Teach Dancing Mexicans love to dance and are experts at salsa, merengue and traditional steps. Hire a couple of skilled local dancers who can travel with you to tourist destinations to stage some public dance classes. All you need is a boom box and possibly a plastic mat showing the dance steps.

Get permission to teach at small hotels or larger resorts. Tourists have fun learning the local steps and acquire a "souvenir" — their ability to salsa — that they can take home with them.

Embroidery Business Buy a single-head embroidery machine that stitches the names or funny sayings your customers want on hats and tee-shirts. Locate your fancy "embroidery cart" in a mall or plaza frequented by national and foreign tourists. Once you get one location up and running, seek out other locations in hot tourist spots.

Dating Service Offer a respectable service that introduces serious-minded, native-English-speaking men and women to their foreign counterparts in Mexico. E-mail and video technology could enable your customers to communicate with their prospective mates. A quality World Wide Web page to market your compmay's services is a must. This latest technology offers new possibilities in this field.

Sales Representative This business could put you on both sides of the border. Start a company that represents foreign-brand products that could be sold in the Mexican marketplace, as well as Mexican products with a market in the U.S. or Canada. Finding the right distributor or buyer is the exporter's biggest challenge. Become an agent to put buyers in touch with sellers on either side of the border.

Find a reliable company that has a quality product that you feel the consumers in your target country will buy. Next, arm yourself with product samples and hit the pavement looking for potential buyers or distributors. Mexican and U.S. trade shows are a good starting point. Work out a commission for each sale or a flat fee for each deal you negotiate in advance.

Or buy the product yourself at a big discount and resell it to interested foreign buyers.

START-UPS FOR LESS THAN $10,000

Colonial Towns The tourist potential of Mexico's fabulous coastline has long been discovered, but the country's interior offers something most beach resorts can't — genuine Mexican culture. Small colonial towns, such as San Miguel de Allende and Guanajuato, offer an ethnic view of Mexico in a picturesque, tranquil setting that will have people coming back again and again. The country's colonial towns could be Mexico's best kept secret. They're brimming with opportunity in all investment sectors, from tourism and manufacturing to services and importing/exporting.

Offer tours of a colonial town that has been overlooked by mainstream tour operators and travel books. Then set up gift shops, money exchange and other services catering to your tourists. A good example might be the beautiful and historic town of Dolores Hidalgo, which is located only one hour from the most popular colonial town of them all, San Miguel de Allende.

Telemarketing Only 40 registered companies are dedicated solely to telemarketing services in Mexico. Of these, only five operate more than 50 workstations — some of the biggest marketing companies in the U.S. have more than 10,000 workstations.

Telemarketing is one of the fastest-growing industries within the direct marketing field, according to Jeff Wright in the magazine *Business Mexico*. Wright admits that market size is still undefined, but a telemarketing explosion over the past two years now has more than 70 percent of medium-to-large companies using telemarketing is some way.

Take some of the "tried and true" business techniques used by U.S. telemarketers and apply those secrets in Mexico. Start small by concentrating on one industry and expand to other areas and industries as demand grows. Mexico's less-than-perfect phone lines and telecommunications infrastructure will be your biggest challenge.

A laundrymat can be an inexpensive and very successful business in Mexico, particularly in tourist areas.

Specialized Tours or Eco Tours It takes a little creativity to start a tour for less that $10,000, but it can be done. Try a tour that takes future expats or investors around to popular gringo living and investment areas, showing them real estate, shopping areas and government buildings where they can get their residency or driver's license. Show them what living in Mexico is really like and some good investment opportunities while you're at it.

To reduce operating expenses, take Mexico's excellent and inexpensive first-class buses around the country to the popular living areas. The tour can also familiarize newcomers with everyday things, like eating in restaurants, taking the bus and taxi, renting or buying a house. You'll find that many real estate agents, attorneys and business consultants would be happy to meet with your group.

Or what about going into business with nature. Take small groups to Mexico's Yucatan Peninsula to view its fabulous ruins and pyramids. Or head down to Belize, the small and distinctly different, English-speaking country that borders Mexico to the south, only a bus ride from Cancún or a short flight from other parts of Mexico. Belize is also a popular country for North American expats. Combine business with pleasure through a fact-finding, tourism excursion.

Mail Order Here's another idea we can thank the Internet for. Open a service that obtains hard-to-find products like new books, innovative hardware products or even certain food items, and make them available through the mail to customers on the opposite side of the border.

English and Spanish School In the larger cities and towns you will find plenty of excellent language schools that have been around forever. But what about in the smaller towns and newer tourist areas like Bahías de Huatulco or parts of Baja California. It's best to service both the locals, by offering English lessons, and the foreigners, by offering Spanish lessons. Teach the English classes yourself until the school gets going. Later, hire reliable Mexicans to teach the Spanish classes for a reasonable fee.

It's important to set up a "home stay" program where your foreign students can live with a Mexican family to get the most out of living and learning the culture, customs and language. Find a location that is far enough away from the rest of the language schools, but close enough that it's easy to get to. If the area is noted for some special natural attractions, so much the better! A school located in ethnic Mexico, away from the tourist locations like Guadalajara or Puerto Vallarta is a big advantage to the serious student who really wants to learn.

Multi-Level Marketing (MLM) Mexico's lack of distribution infrastructure opens the door for alternative methods of reaching "Joe public." MLM has been around the U.S. and Canada forever but is relatively new in Mexico. Huge multinationals like Amway and Mary Kay Cosmetics have been here for some time, but what about starting a company that offers new and different products. A small company can take advantage of niches the big ones don't cover.

Create a network of hard-working locals who go door to door offering products that are affordable and in demand. Your job would be to supply the product on consignment to your independent employees, and meet with them weekly to collect their earnings and deliver more merchandise.

Laundry Mat Open a small one, with a few machines and some good contacts. You could install a coin-operated cleaners or hire cheap labor to service your customers. Locate in a area with plenty of tourist traffic. Hotels and restaurants could give you their commercial accounts. Once you're overseeing two or three laundry mats in good locations, the profits could come rolling in.

Translation and Typing Service Dependable, fast and precise typing, translation and interpreting services are often in short supply in Mexico, but are vital for the company looking to expand abroad or the foreigner needing help with official translations.

Good interpreting equipment and a reputation for quality can secure government contracts to provide translation services during diplomatic events. Well-educated, bilingual nationals, already skilled in typing and translating, are ready to work for wages that are low by U.S. standards. Entrepreneurs seeking to establish this type of business don't necessarily need to know Spanish or even have typing skills to become successful, but strong management and marketing skills, as well as a little hustle, are a must.

Handicrafts, Clothing and Exporting Mexico's beautiful pottery, wood carvings, clothing, silver and turquoise jewelry, white-wood furniture, embroidery, rugs, leather articles, blown glass and other crafts practically sell themselves. Big opportunities exist for handicraft exporters in hungry foreign markets. The country's highest quality handicrafts are sold for next to nothing here, but the same merchandise fetches hefty prices in U.S. and Canadian boutiques. The key is to find a reliable, high-volume manufacturer and low-cost, insured transportation out of the country. Mexico offers a bevy of incentives to the industrial exporter of goods assembled in-country under the temporary admission system and then exported to the world market. A clever small-time exporter, with some key contacts abroad, can profit by marketing Mexico's native products to the world.

Import Mexican's love to eat U.S. foods and wear U.S. clothing. With a sizable middle and upper class and a foreign population of more than 500,000, importers are not hard-pressed to develop a loyal clientele. Try to gain exclusive rights to import goods that can be complemented by a wide range of related products. A good knowledge of Spanish and customs laws will help a lot here. If you want a little tip on this one, contact Wal-Mart or Sears international division. You may be able to place your product with these world-class buyers.

Furniture and Wood Products Mexico is internationally known for its fine, hand-made wood furnishings, wrought-iron sculptures, carved stone and other handicrafts. A trip through any of the country's colonial towns will reveal world-class crafts and furnishings at rock-bottom prices. The trick is finding an artisan who provides high quality work and reliable service.

Business Services Both NAFTA and state privatization efforts are creating great demand for staff education, quality control consulting, data processing, office support and market research. Mexican executives are becoming increasingly aware that without these vital services, they will not be able to keep up with their aggressive, well-informed foreign competitors.

START-UPS FOR $10,000 AND UP

Mini-Storage Units Mexican families aren't as mobile as their North American counterparts, but as the middle class grows and more foreign professionals relocate, temporary storage of furnishings will become more in demand. Mini-storage units are almost non-existent in this country, which has three times the population of California. Many export companies temporarily need storage space before shipping their goods out.

In Mexico City, where space is like gold, some businesses would also pay a little extra per month for additional storage space for important documents, filing cabinets and more. And many foreigners living in Mexico will probably need some type of storage space for cars, boats or furnishings when between houses. Don't forget about embassy employees. They are constantly moving throughout Mexico and may find temporary storage very useful.

Bookstores The English language bookstore has always been a favorite hang out for sociable expatriates in a foreign land, yet only a few of these stores exist in Mexico City and in Guadalajara. Plenty of opportunity is out there for the innovative entrepreneur who imports foreign reading material. The coffee-shop atmosphere of many famous North American bookstores has yet to arrive in Mexico. The concept would provide expatriates and cultured nationals with an irresistible mix of culture, conversation and a great cup of coffee.

Used Car Rentals Mexican rent-a-car companies charge an astounding $50.00 per day plus mileage for their least expensive vehicle. All the proper insurance and infrastructure exist here to provide used cars for rent. Even a minimal fleet of three or four vehicles can bring in $2,000 to $3,000 per month. The disadvantages of upkeep and repairs make this business best suited to car buffs.

Low Income Housing Mexico's housing deficit of more than 6 million units and annual construction rate of only 350,000 offer a golden opportunity for the construction entrepreneur. Banks offer little permanent financing and construction loans, so business start up will require lots of cash. The most popular homes of two to three bedrooms have been selling for between $30,000 and $50,000 in big city suburbs. Be ready to take back a mortgage or try to pre-sell before you build. Even though the economy is at an ebb, many Mexicans have money and want to own their own homes.

New and Used Furniture Rental The up-and-down economy has forced many unprepared companies into bankruptcy, and blow-out sales on office furnishings and equipment are common. This offers a unique opportunity for resellers who target new small-to-medium size businesses. The service would also appeal to the multi-national corporation not wanting to invest a lot of capital in overseas start-up.

Real Estate Companies Many large residential and commercial real estate franchises and small, independently owned foreign companies have been operating successfully for years in Mexico. Recent changes in the law regarding rural property ownership and the liberalization of the 1993 Foreign Investment Law should spur a surge of interest in these once prohibited properties.

Insurance Fewer than four million Mexicans carry life insurance, only 2 percent buy homeowners policies and a mere 25 percent purchase car insurance. Mexico is now considered the top insurance market in Latin America. Under NAFTA, all equity and market share restrictions will be eliminated by 2000, opening the market to private insurance agents. Success in this sector will mean active marketing to educate Mexicans about the need for insurance, as well as an aggressive sales program for new and existing multi-national corporations. Car insurance is optional in Mexico, but new laws are in the works to make this insurance mandatory.

Gambling Gambling is still illegal in Mexico, but with the economic slump, the government is looking for new ways to generate foreign capital. The legalization of gambling is being considered. Big names in the business, including Steve Wynn, Circus Circus and Donald Trump, are already eyeing possible Mexican locations. Gambling would be the biggest investment move Mexico has made in the last 50 years and would give an important boost to the hotel, restaurant and tourist industry. Watch and listen for this one.

Medical Supplies The medical supply and equipment business has surged in recent years. Even with the peso devaluation, sales in the industry are off only 15 percent, and this figure should improve dramatically as the economy recovers. The current administration of President Ernesto Zedillo has announced plans to overhaul the socialized medicine system by creating privately run pension funds and joint ventures with U.S. partners to compete with the state system. This should spur unprecedented demand for new equipment and supplies to meet the country's growing needs.

Textiles and Apparel Tremendous opportunity exists for the foreign entrepreneur willing to become a joint venture partner with a Mexican textile and apparel company. Thousands of small Mexican companies need modern, automated machinery to compete in the strong export market. Also, many family "micro" operations can use advice about how to channel their merchandise to the outside world.

Franchises The new, open business climate, reduced government restrictions and streamlined registration process have combined to create conditions that have never been more favorable for the foreign franchisee. With more than 70 percent of the population living in urban areas, Mexico is ideal for the vendor of U.S. products, services and foods. Many North American franchises already operate here. Franchises in hot demand include weight-control centers, exercise spas, movie theaters, athletic shoe outlets, copy centers, business services and fast food restaurants.

Bed and Breakfast Mexico is filled with good, low-priced hotels and bed and breakfasts. Competition is tough in this sector but opportunity exists for innovators. One popular B&B in Ensenada is more like a low-end Club Med. For one price they offer all the beer, margaritas and food you can eat, in a ranch setting with horse back riding and swimming. None of the rustic, old cabins have locks, and guests are permitted to enter the kitchen at all hours of the night to make sandwiches or just hang out.

Locate close to the border or to a large city to attract both foreigners and nationals who are looking for something a little crazy and different. Sites near majestic volcanoes or indigenous ruins would also be an attraction. Once the word gets out, your customers will do your marketing for you by telling their family and friends.

Hand Car Wash Saturday morning in Mexico finds literally all car owners out in their driveways scrubbing and honing their vehicles to a fine shine. The country offers a few hand-wash and vacuum locations, but this could be an interesting opportunity in this car-loving nation.

Arcade Fun Centers Mexico's young population, with a penchant for family life, makes the country a prime location for water parks, miniature golf, go-cart tracks, arcades and more. Security-conscious parents want their children to have a safe, clean place to play. Locate in a mall or near popular shopping areas where parents can drop off their kids while they shop. Excellent potential here.

Executive Offices Deluxe office space could be a lucrative investment, depending on the locations and the services offered.

Offices should be within easy driving distance of an airport and near one of Mexico's larger business centers. Services offered should include translation, telephone answering and message-taking, fax, computers and e-mail. The center could cut costs by offering collective secretaries and by locating an international courier drop box on-site.

FRANCHISE BUSINESS

U.S. franchisers are eager to expand to lucrative Latin markets. Mexicans like U.S. goods and services, and franchises have been highly successful here. The U.S. and Mexico's shared border improves communication and lowers shipping costs.

Positive changes in Mexico's Foreign Investment Law, government support of the franchise concept and a huge demand for U.S. goods and services all combine to make the franchise a lucrative investment possibility. Set-up procedures have been streamlined and much red-tape removed. NAFTA now provides the important patent protection many franchisers seek before investing abroad.

Most franchises locate in high-population centers, such as Guadalajara, Monterrey, the popular border areas and Mexico City, where more than 20 million people live. Some of the better-known franchises operating in Mexico include Mail Boxes Etc., Subway, Blockbuster Videos, Kwik Kopy's and Century 21 Real Estate.

How to Get Started Before embarking upon any investment in Mexico, do your homework. It's vitally important to find a local business partner with ample business and cultural experience. A trustworthy partner and manager could make the difference between profit and total loss.

Visit the local branch of the American Chamber of Commerce and talk to as many people as possible in related fields. This will require at least one extended stay in-country before start-up can begin. International business expos can also provide valuable information. Foreign governments often share a favorable view of franchising because it means revenue and jobs for local people. Advertise in business journals for potential partners, but thoroughly check out a prospective co-investor before signing a contract.

Keeping tabs on your business is an important factor, especially if you live abroad. Study the market carefully before deciding on a salable product or service. Consider the logistics of quality control, hiring of staff, and operation before you invest. Computer technology can help you with control, but it's no substitute for a dependable "right hand" man or woman.

For up-to-date information about international markets, subscribe to an on-line service, such as CompuServe, America Online, Prodigy and Delphi Internet Services Corp. But spend time in the country and do hands-on research. Read the local phone books, get to know the people and the culture, determine your business niche, and then decide if a Mexican investment is for you.

The list on the next page of U.S. franchises seeking locations in Latin America should give you a good start on your search.

IT TAKES TIME

One of the more frustrating concepts encountered by the new entrepreneur in Mexico is the term "ahorita" (ah-or-EE-tah). Loosely translated as "pretty soon," when you hear that something will happen "ahorita," it could mean within the next five minutes or even the next two hours.

Business takes a little longer here. Your Mexican associates will want to know who you are, not just what you need from them. Up to two-hour lunches may seem inefficient to the U.S. or Canadian investor, but it's the Mexican way and should be respected. The extra time spent getting acquainted teaches the newcomer how business is done here and, eventually, how to speed things up...*a la mexicana.*

FRANCHISE POSSIBILITIES

No.	FRANCHISE	FAX	DESCRIPTION
1.	Subway	203 876-6688	Submarine sandwiches, salads
2.	Dairy Queen	612 830-0450	Soft serve daily products/sandwiches
3.	Jani-King	214 991-5723	Commercial cleaning services
4.	Chem-Dry	801 755-0021	Carpet cleaning/fabric care
5.	Electronic Reality Associates	913 491-9133	Real estate services
6.	Tower Cleaning Systems	610 293-9985	Office cleaning services
7.	The Medicine Shoppe	314-995-6334	Pharmacy
8.	Popeyes Chicken & Biscuits	404 353-3170	Fried chicken & biscuits
9.	Merry Maids	402 498-0142	Residential cleaning
10.	Miracle Ear	612 520-9520	Hearing aids
11.	Fantastic Sam's	901 363-8946	Hair salons
12.	Money Mailer	714 265-4091	Direct-mail advertising
13.	Minuteman Press Int'l. Inc.	516 249-5618	Full-service printing center
14.	One Hour Martinizing Dry Cleaning	513 731-5513	Dry cleaning services
15.	Kwik Kopy Corp.	713 373-4450	Printing & copying services
16.	Decorating Den	301 652-9017	Interior decorating
17.	Applebee's Neighborhood Grill & Bar	913 341-1694	Restaurant
18.	Travel Network	201 567-4405	Travel agency
19.	Kampgrounds of America Inc.	406 248-7414	Campgrounds
20.	Travel Agents Int'l. Inc.	813 579-0529	Travel agency
21.	Sbarro The Italian Factory	516 462-9165	Italian food
22.	Check Express USA Inc.	813 223-4308	Check cashing/related services
23.	Together Dating Service	508 872-7679	Personal-introduction services
24.	Speedy Sign-A-Rama USA	407 640-5580	Full-service sign business
25.	The Maids-Americas Maids Service	402 558-4112	Residential cleaning
26.	AlphaGraphics Printshops	602 887-2850	Printing services
27.	Microplay Video Games	905 949-4516	Video game stores
28.	Pak Mail Centers of America Inc.	303 755-9721	Packing/shipping/business support
29.	Dr. Vinyl & Associates Ltd.	816 478-3065	Vinyl/windshield repair
30.	SuperGlass Windshield Repair	404 734-0815	Windshield repair
31.	Pretzelmaker Inc.	303 573-0004	Pretzels
32.	The Taco Maker	801 621-0139	Mexican fast food
33.	USA Baby	708 832-0139	Kid's furniture & accessories
34.	Gourmet Cup	708 735-0244	Coffees, teas & accessories
35.	Water Mart	602 926-6463	Retail water stores
36.	Roll-A-Way	813-579-9410	Rolling security and shutters
37.	Pet Nanny	517 694-5113	In-home pet care

Source: Entrepreneur Magazine

A WORD OF CAUTION

Even for an experienced investor, it's a mistake to think that a successful venture in Mexico will be easy. It's best to take the Murphy's Law approach and try to anticipate problems before they arise. The only way to do this is through research and extended personal visits before embarking on a major investment.

All business owners will tell you that it takes twice as much money to open a business as they had originally thought, and twice as much time to do some typical daily transactions, such as banking. Research and patience are your best defenses.

Possible obstacles include: faulty or sporadic telephone or electricity service, many national holidays, long bank and post office lines, cumbersome bureaucracy, minimum bank financing, language and culture clashes, and finding trustworthy and skilled employees. Also, a strong tendency to "put off until tomorrow" just about any activity — no matter how urgent — is endemic in some cultures. Talk to everyone you can and do your research before opening a business.

Selected payoffs to certain corrupt government officials may help speed some aspects of a project, but it is specially important that the foreign investor "play by the rules." All local tax laws must be followed and proper permits obtained and renewed. It is important to hire the services of a good attorney, skilled in cutting through the red tape. Not to do so will eventually jeopardize your investment.

THE FINAL WORD

Starting a business in Mexico is tough. Bureaucracy and infrastructure problems try the patience of even experienced entrepreneurs. Those who succeed here not only have a keen business sense, but also genuinely love the culture and people. Before making up your mind to set up a business in Mexico, make sure you spend some time here. If the lifestyle isn't for you, the business world probably won't be either.

THE PEOPLE WHO'VE DONE IT

Throughout Mexico you will find many U.S. and Canadian citizens who have prospered in business by starting small and building their business into a regional, national or international contender.

The following pages contain stories of these people who are living and working in Mexico right now. Their practical experiences, tips and secrets to success are invaluable and can't be learned from any text book. But before we get into their individual profiles, let us take a minute or two to really emphasize some of their most important tips and tricks — some of them may surprise you.

For example, most of these people agree that finding financing to start a business is easier abroad then back home — but not from any bank. Many successful overseas entrepreneurs find the start-up capital they need just by networking with other, wealthier, expats who are willing to take a risk on a good idea.

These "investment angles" might be retirees who want to keep busy doing something, but not on a full-time basis, or part-time expatriates who live in Mexico only long enough to get out of the cold northern winters, one day hoping to live there, year-round. And don't rule out the Mexicans! Many are looking for a foreign partner experienced in dealing with the foreign resident population and tourists.

Finding these angles can be as easy as frequenting many of the popular expat hang-outs, like the American Legion, investment clubs, the Rotary Club, Republicans or Democrats Abroad or the Kiwanis Club, to name a few. If you are an honest, hardworking individual with good ideas and a strong desire to succeed, finding the money could be the easiest part of starting a business in Mexico.

"Follow up is a big part of my day"
Katie Reeder
Ajijic Exports

Canadian, Spencer Shulman, 35, found the financing to start his popular chicken restaurant in San Antonio de Tlycapan in Paul Rutledge, a retired U.S. citizen living there. Rutledge had restaurant experience and a sizable bank account, and Shulman had the desire to learn the business and perseverance to make it succeed.

Or, take Katie Reeder, a 25-year-old furniture exporter from La Jolla, California, who told us, "I just didn't like any of the opportunities available to me after graduation. I wanted something more exciting." Katie considered her Stateside options, and then chose Mexico. At first, Katie's family and friends thought she was crazy, but now they envy her international lifestyle.

Most expat businessmen and women live in Mexico year-round, returning home for quick Christmas visits or summer breaks. It is practically impossible, they've discovered, to start and maintain a business without staying actively involved in the everyday process. It becomes a lot easier to wake up to the warm, Mexican sun everyday, than confront a harsh, northern winter!

But many entrepreneurs try to start a business in Mexico that they can leave for a couple months a year, in case of illness or family emergency back home.

The Internet has been a boon to many foreign business owners in Mexico. When we stopped in to talk with David Merryman from Omaha, Nebraska at his Remax real estate franchise, he had a stack of e-mail that had come in that day from North Americans and Europeans interested in investing in Mexico. And his web site gets hundreds of hits a week. In the case of Merryman and many others, e-mail, Internet phone and videoconferencing will increasingly play an important role in their business.

"Even after being here five years, everyday is still a learning experience"

Spencer Shulman
Chicken Little Restaurant

Some of our interviewees preferred to start off by buying a small, existing business. An existing business will free up your time and pay your bills, enabling you to become acquatinted with Mexican culture and customs. Existing businesses also presumably have all their required licenses and operation permits, eliminating one of the most frustrating and time-consuming start-up procedures for the newcomer. With permits in place, relocation or expansion becomes easier.

Most wish they'd brought more money with them, because unexpected start-up expenses often caused their initial budgets to soar. Some have also warned us about the dangers of being too inflexible about the type of business to start — they, themselves, arrived in Mexico with specific ideas in mind, but now, two or three businesses later, they've finally found their niche.

Don't let the language stop you. Although we strongly suggest that you make a concentrated, on-going effort to learn Spanish, fluency isn't necessary for success. Vickey Laurie Sclisizzi, a woman we know from Ontario, Canada, became a successful restaurateur despite her rudimentary Spanish.

It's not a bad idea to work for someone else for a while, until you feel more comfortable with Mexico. Several of the success stories we've come across in Mexico began this way to gain experience and settle in before launching a business of their own.

Sean Godfrey from Colorado worked at the local English-language newspaper, The Colony Reporter, as an advertising sales rep before he and his English partner ended up buying the paper when it came up for sale. "Without the prior years of running a newspaper in Mexico it would have been next to impossible to succeed and grow as quickly as we did," Godfrey told us.

Starting and running a business in Mexico is not easy. It takes a lot of determination, innovation, dedication and all the qualities that entrepreneurs must have back home. Our sources tell us that in a foreign country you need to be *more* committed and *even better* prepared. But if you stick it out, the rewards are many.

The camaraderie of Mexico's expat business community is apparent. Although from many backgrounds and just as many countries, successful expats share one common characteristic: their genuine respect and admiration for the people of Mexico and things Mexican. Even old-timers will tell you of the excitement they feel everyday as they wake up.

PROFILE OF THE TYPICAL
NORTH AMERICAN EXPAT BUSINESS OWNER

* **Age:** 28 to 55 years.
* **Capital brought down:** $15,000 (Average).
* **Reason for coming**: Opportunities, climate, culture and people.
* **Biggest mistake**: Should have brought more start-up capital.
* **Best advice when starting a business**: Be prepared. Try to anticipate.
* **Visits home**: Approximately two weeks a year.
* **Key to success**: Accepting the Mexican culture and people.

TAKE OUR TIPS

The following are more tips and inside secrets that we have uncovered from interviews with successful expatriates in Mexico:

Follow the money Pick a business in which your target customer is the tourist or the expat as protection from Mexico's turbulent peso devaluations, recessions and inflation. If you're dealing with

> *"Outsourcing work motivates workers to do better work then having permanent employees."*
> Rod Collins
> Southmex.com

foreigners, you only need to raise your prices to keep up with your standard of living. This becomes impossible when your target customer is Mexican, who is subject to frequent salary devaluations. But be cautious during the off season, when expats return home after the northern winter or during the low tourist season.

Good employees Finding trained, honest and hard-working employees is one of the most difficult hurdles faced by business owners in Mexico. Spend extra time finding the right employees and pay them a little extra. Conscientious employees can sometimes "mind the store" and give you the time to concentrate on expanding, improving or spending more time at the beach!

The more control the better Choose a business that doesn't require many employees or outside help. If you want to build homes, for example, be prepared for dozens of subcontractors with dozens of employees — completing just one house could be a nightmare! If you choose an exporting business, by contrast, you may only be dealing with the manufacture of your product and the shipping company. At start-up time, fewer is better.

Don't expect much help from business chambers or consulates These organizations are set up to help the large multinational company. They may be able to give you some good contacts and help with some general business questions, but don't expect much.

Some experience is helpful Learning a new business in a foreign country can be very difficult. We highly recommend starting a business in Mexico at which you already have some experience. Knowing what you're getting into is a key to success.

Seek a Mexican partner It is not necessary by law to have a Mexican partner, but a dependable country national can really smooth the way with employee relations, cultural matters and government red tape. When General Motors introduced the Chevy Nova to Mexican markets, even their experts failed to catch that "Nova" or "*No va*" in Spanish means "It doesn't go" — not the kind of name that would make the average Mexican want to run out and buy the car!

Service Quality service will pay off. All North Americans and other foreigners from industrialized nations, as well as well-traveled Mexicans, will gladly pay a little extra for a quality service. Remember it!

Red Tape Bureaucracy and red tape will add at least 30 percent to your bottom line. Even with low employee wages, state-mandated health, social security and other benefits can add another 15 to 25 percent to the hourly rate.

The Mordida The *mordida* translates literally as "the bite," but it's the word Mexicans use to describe the bribe paid to people in authority to help you get things done quicker. Paying a *mordida* may help speed things along, but you shouldn't use it to sidestep laws or regulations.

Go slow Mexico is not the place for get-rich-quick schemes.

"Newcomers should work for someone for at least two years before pursing their own venture."
Sean Godfrey
Colony Reporter

Building a business takes more time than in North America and is based more on personal relationships and socializing.

So, without further adieu, here they are — the Captains of small industry in Mexico. Read their profiles carefully and learn from their experiences. If you manage to start and maintain a successful business in Mexico, it probably won't be long before we come knocking on your door too.

DAVID MERRYMAN

When we stopped by David's office it was busy with walk-in clients, mainly retirees from the U.S. and Canada looking for housing. The majority of his agents are fellow North Americans, who, like him, ended up in the town of Lake Chapala, on the banks of Mexico's largest lake, attracted by the year-round perfect climate, friendly people and low-cost living.

Name: David Merryman
From: Omaha, Nebraska
Residence:
Chapala, Jalisco
Business Name:
Remax Lake Chapala

Business Description: Real estate sales, rentals , management, construction and re-modeling.

Why Mexico? Having checked out living and business opportunities in various Latin countries, I found that Mexico had 1) the friendliest people 2) the best climate, and 3) a favorable cost of living. You really have the best of both worlds.

How did you get started? I immigrated to Mexico at the age of 42 and knew that I would have to engage in some sort of business activity as I was too young to retire. I chose the construction and real estate business because it seemed to have a promising future.

Keys to Success: Accepting the culture of Mexico, patience, are all the virtues that any entrepreneur anywhere in the world needs — hard work, honesty and concern for your customers.

KATIE REEDER

When we stopped to talk to Katie in her beautifully decorated showroom, she apologized for not having a lot of inventory on hand because she'd just finished redecorating a big house in the area. She has the only store in her community that can do complete interior decoration and fill special hard-to-find orders. At 25, she is the youngest expat we interviewed.

Name: Katie Reeder
From: La Jolla, California
Residence:
Ajijic, Jalisco, Mexico
Business Name:
Ajijic Exports

Business Description: Exporting, consulting, and decorating with furniture accessories and art.

Why Mexico? I always wanted to work with Mexico, originally from the U.S. At first I thought I would stay only a short time, but now I like it better here.

How did you get started? I worked as an intern for one year with Associated Merchandising Corporation in Mexico. I left to start my own business, first working out of my house using my contacts, a fax machine and a lap-top computer. I then obtained financing from a contact I'd made to open a 2,000 sq. ft showroom.

Key to success: It is essential to speak Spanish and to adapt to the culture. The biggest part of my time is constantly making business contacts and following-up to make sure things get done. A big part of living in Mexico is giving back to the community. One way I do this is to buy my inventory from local vendors. I don't feel that being a woman has negatively affected me here in business.

ROD COLLINS

Rod's office, filled with the latest computer technology, looks more like a high tech office in Silicon Valley, not small-town Mexico. But the information age has arrived in Mexico, and people like Rod are working hard to fill the increasing needs of nationals and expats seeking to incorporate the latest tools into their businesses to compete on a global level.

Name: Rod Collins
From: Holtville, California
Residence: Chapala
Business Name: Southmex.com

Business Description: Web publishing, ISP (dial-up) and web site hosting. We also help people hook up and repair their computers. Right now the majority of our business is supplying e-mail access to North Americans who want a quick and inexpensive way to contact family and friends.

Why Mexico? I feel I can have a better lifestyle here then in the States. And there are many more business opportunities, more potential for growth and it's a lot less expensive to get a business up and running.

How did you get started? When I first came down to Mexico I ran a family-owned pre-press and printing company. After the '94 peso devaluation, we decided to sell and look for other business opportunities. I saw a lot of potential in the Internet business, so I went back to the States to learn about computers in order to return and start a computer-related business here.

Key to Success: I found that outsourcing work to other companies or individuals will get me better quality than having permanent employees. We currently outsource 70 percent of our work. With the arrival of Internet, we are seeing many more business-oriented people who never would have been able to move to Mexico without it. We see this as one of our biggest future customer-base opportunities.

SEAN GODFREY

Guadalajara is host to the largest North American population outside the U.S. and Canada and Sean is co-owner of the largest English-language newspaper in the city. We were lucky to catch up with him before he left for Puerto Vallarta to check on his paper's distribution and meet with some staff writers. Sean is married to a Mexican doctor.

Name: Sean Godfrey
From: Lived last seven U.S. years in Colorado, working and studying.
Residence: Guadalajara
Business Name: The Colony Reporter

Business Description: A weekly English-language newspaper that provides North Americans, Canadians and others living in Guadalajara, Chapala, Puerto Vallarta and abroad news in English about their communities and regional, state and national news.

Why Mexico? Came as a student. I met my wife here, and we decided to stay and find work.

How Did You Get Started? My first experience at the Colony Reporter was with the business end of things. I left to start a tourist-related paper in Mazatlan, which didn't work out. I returned to Guadalajara and decided to buy the Colony Reporter with a fellow employee when it came up for sale in 1994.

Key to success: My partner Michael Forbes and I bought the paper at a time when circulation was low due to management problems. We turned it around by updating our computers and graphic art department and by hiring some top-notch reporters. We have stayed focused on our readers. We noticed that our readership is changing from retirees to 40-to-50-year-olds who aren't yet ready to retire. I highly recommend that newcomers work for a few years to gain experience with the culture and language before going off on their own.

SPENCER SHULMAN

Spencer is considered the ultimate entrepreneur because of his side businesses — car repairs and land development to name just two — and Mexico is an ideal place for a guy with Spencer's energy. He lives with his Canadian wife who works at a local real estate office and their four Labrador Retrievers.

Name: Spencer Shulman
From: Canada
Residence: Mojonera, Jalisco
Business Name: Chicken Little

Shulman (left) with partner José Navarro

Business Description: We have a sit-down restaurant that serves chicken cooked many different ways and comes with beans, rice etc. We filled a niche in the market by providing the local restaurants with chicken prepared and ready-to-cook. Before, they had to buy the whole chicken, feathers and all. We also sell fresh chicken to the public.

Why Mexico? I came in '92 to get involved in a business opportunity before NAFTA.

How did you get started? Forty five days after I arrived, I bought a little corner store for $5,000. I started this way in order to learn the culture, the people and the way business is done in Mexico while I covered my living expenses. I sold the store for a nice little profit and then got a job selling advertising space for a local newspaper where I worked for two years. I then met my two partners, José Navarro, a Mexican, and American Paul Rutledge and we got the chicken restaurant going.

Key to success: When we first opened, we grew so fast we had to expand three times in a 18-month period. I contribute this to providing our customers, which are 90 percent foreigners, with what they want — a place that is clean and affordable, with incredibly tasty food. The majority of my success I contribute to picking the right business partners.

TOM THOMPSON

Business-savvy Tom Thompson is owner of not one, but three successful businesses. Tom's secret to success seems to be in knowing what the people want, and giving it to them. It's obvious that the employees at Tom's Bazaar respect him — very important when you're running three businesses.

Name: Tom Thompson
From: San Diego, California
Residence: Ajijic, Jalisco
Business Names:
Barbara's Bazaar, La Colección
Barbara, Porta Libros

Business Description: We have a popular, English-language used-book store that mainly sells to the expatriates living in the area. Our bazaar sells everything from used furniture, household goods and old records to photos and everything else. Our La Colección Barbara has antiques and Persian rugs. We do estate sales and appraisals.

Why Mexico? I retired in 1984 from a similar business in San Diego, known as the "Prop Shop." I spent nine years on sabbatical in the coastal village of Yelapa. In 1993 I moved to Ajijic because of the near perfect climate.

How did you get started? I happened upon another gringo who was selling an existing business, similar to my Bazaar. Buying an existing business with all the permits in place and a little inventory gave me a head start over starting from scratch. It also was easier for me to expand from one location doing one activity to three locations doing three different activities with an already approved license.

Key To Success: Understanding the culture in order to develop a staff of cooperative employees. Being fair and honest with my customers in this small village has had tremendous positive results. In small communities around Mexico, word-of-mouth is the only advertising you need.

VICKI LAURIE SCLISIZZI

Ask anyone in the town of Ajijic for a good place to eat lunch or dinner, and most will point you to Sclisizzi's Bruno's 2. When Vicki first arrived in Mexico in 1994 with her young son, she had no idea what Mexico had in store for her. She now lives in a quaint Mexican neighborhood and her 5-year-old son is comfortably settled in school and fluent in Spanish. During working hours she has a neighborhood lady come to the house for $15.00 a week to clean and watch her son. The majority of her customers are North Americans, but she's working hard to attract locals in anticipation of the slow season when the majority of foreigners return home.

Name:
Vicki Laurie Sclisizzi
From: Toronto, Canada
Residence: Aijijic, Jalisco
Business Name: Bruno's 2

Business Description: We serve popular American-style foods like pork chops, bake potatoes and salads, prepared using our own special secret recipes.

Why Mexico? Because it was financially possible to start and run a business here; it's as simple as that. In Canada it's almost impossible to start a small business with limited funds.

How did you get started? My father was my mentor. He owns Bruno's 1, and I was able to learn a lot about the restaurant business from him.

Key to success: The main quality a business owner in Mexico needs is persistence. I also maintain a good relationship with my employees by treating them like family and helping, when I am able to.

BANKING

The Mexican financial system and commercial banking system have undergone radical changes in recent years to become more modern and efficient.

Former President Carlos Salinas privatized Mexico's commercial banks in 1991 and 1992. Today, majority private ownership of capital is permitted in all the country's institutions. The nation's central bank, Banco de México, was established as an autonomous entity of the government with the primary purpose of preserving the purchasing power of the peso. The North American Free Trade Agreement (NAFTA) diversified the Mexican financial system even further by introducing U.S. and Canadian commercial institutions.

The electronic age of banking is slowing creeping across the border, but Mexico still has a long way to go. Perhaps one of the most worrisome aspects of life here is managing your money.

Before setting up shop abroad, discuss your plans with your local bank to find out how it can be of assistance. Your bank can possibly provide you with a letter of introduction, addressed to a correspondent bank in Mexico, that vouches for your signature and provides general references and a written guarantee for checks cashed against the home bank.

Most banks can wire money anywhere in the world, but be sure to research the requisites for a transfer before you leave the country. Many future expats obtain a personal line of credit and increase the limits on their credit cards before they leave home to provide them with the capital they'll need to set up shop abroad.

Be sure to bring your ATM card. No matter where you travel in Mexico, you're bound to come across a Star or Plus bank machine. These are the easiest means to withdraw money from accounts back home, but don't expect dollars. For a fee, ATM machines in Mexico will give you the equivalent of your dollar withdrawal in pesos at the current exchange rate.

Bring travelers checks and cash. A sufficient number of U.S. travelers checks in different denominations is best until you settle in. Any amount of cash or checks may be transported into and out of the U.S., but amounts over $10,000 will have to be registered on special customs form 4790.

Wait until you get to Mexico to exchange dollars into pesos — the exchange rate is better there. As a good rule of thumb, only buy the pesos you'll need to cover traveling expenses. The dollar, because it holds its value much better, is a safer currency for savings. You'll lose money through devaluation if you have to convert pesos back to dollars later.

TRANSACTIONS

With the exception of border zones, where dollar accounts may be permitted, *Mexican banks only permit accounts in pesos.* However, things are slowly changing. At press time, Banco Bancomer was starting to offer dollar accounts with deposits of $5,000 or more. You must first have a peso account that is at least six months old. Most foreigners are still wary of dollar accounts, because in 1982 the government took control of all banks and converted all dollar accounts into pesos at a fraction of the dollar's true value.

Ordinary banking services are otherwise similar to the U.S. and Canadian systems, including savings and checking accounts, combined checking/savings accounts, certificates of deposit, safety deposit boxes, automatic teller machine cards and credit cards.

The combined checking/savings accounts require a higher minimum balance, but pay a higher rate of interest and include a debit card that can be used in restaurants and stores throughout Mexico. This service is particularly handy given that most commercial establishments don't accept personal checks.

At press time, interest rates on peso savings accounts hovered at 15 percent. Savings are insured by the government, and banks are not permitted to fail. No depositor has ever lost principal or interest in a Mexican bank.

Certificates of deposit pay higher interest rates than the combined checking/savings accounts. CDs are offered for various terms, but the most common is the 28-day deposit, which pays around 20 percent per year. The CD has been a popular investment tool for all expatriates, but especially those on a fixed income. Unlike the U.S., however, Mexican CDs cannot be liquidated prior to their date of maturity.

Foreigners must have an FM-2 or FM-3 resident status in order to open a bank account in Mexico (see Residency section for more information). Banks will require proof of one of these classifications and your in-country address. To solicit a Visa or Mastercard that can be used anywhere in the world, you must provide references from a Mexican company or from an established resident and your bank from abroad, as well as proof of your address in Mexico, such as cancelled telephone receipts or bank statements with your address on them. The credit limit will be determined by your salary. Or, you can simply obtain an international Visa or Mastercard *debit* card that draws directly from your Mexican savings account.

CHANGING MONEY

Money-changing houses or "*casas de cambio*" are everywhere in Mexico and make it easy to obtain pesos. The houses readily exchange foreign currency, travelers checks and Visa or Mastercard transactions for pesos. The larger houses usually work with smaller buy-sell margins, offering a better exchange rate than commercial banks.

Because the peso is a highly unstable currency, most foreigners keep the bulk of their savings in foreign banks abroad, where they are safe from frequent devaluations of the Mexican currency.

Cashing personal checks from a foreign bank usually takes about six weeks. Each check will be charged a service fee of from 1 to 1.5 percent or more of the amount of the transaction. This becomes expensive for those who frequently cash checks drawn from a foreign bank to pay monthly expenses. Most national banks offer wire transfers from foreign banks, but this can take two to three days and may be a little confusing for the non-Spanish speaker. Few Mexican banks have English speaking employees.

TIPS *To side-step this lengthy bureaucracy, the best option is to open a checking account in a U.S. bank that has a relationship with a Mexican bank or open an account with a reputable Mexican investment firm. Smart foreign residents only change two to three months' living expenses into pesos to protect themselves against devaluations.*

One firm popular with the expatriate population is the Allen W. Lloyd Company. A peso account at Lloyd's enables the account holder to cash checks from U.S. and Canadian banks free-of-charge. The company also offers auto and medical insurance, as well as real estate and market funds in pesos at competitive interest rates.

But most important for the foreign investor or retiree, companies like Lloyd's always employ several people who speak English — a big help when dealing with money matters. Contact Lloyd's at Headquarters Office: Mariano Otero 1915, Guadalajara, Jalisco 44560, Mexico. Tel: (3) 121-90-50 or 647-49-86. Fax: (3) 647-21-28.

FRIENDSHIP ACCOUNT

Another favorite bank among expats is the California Commerce Bank, a subsidiary of Mexico's Banamex. Their program is designed for North American senior citizens, 55 years and older, who live in Mexico. Called the "Friendship" senior checking program, the account requires no minimum deposit or balance. You must, however, open a "*Programa Amistad*" account at a Banamex Bank in Mexico to be able to cash checks. Benefits include:

Immediate cash and no-fee check cashing A California Commerce Bank check for the peso equivalent of up to $200 U.S. can be cashed daily free-of-charge at any local branch of Banamex. You'll receive the cash immediately.

Free personalized checks Also free-of-charge, these specially designed checks can be used both as regular U.S.-style checks or for convenient check-cashing throughout Mexico. Account holders are also issued an identification card that facilitates check cashing at Banamex.

U.S. government protection through FDIC insurance Because California Commerce Bank is a U.S. bank with a central office in Los Angeles, checking accounts are insured up to $100,000 per account with the Federal Deposit Insurance Corporation (FDIC). Coverage can be expanded by opening more accounts under the names of family members.

Bonus interest Friendship Senior Checking Account funds earn an extra 1 percent bonus interest over the current rates for regular depositors. The account holder may choose unlimited check-writing privileges or a three check per month limit.

Convenience Checks may be deposited free-of-charge at the nearest Banamex branch using the special program identification card. Banamex is Mexico's largest bank with more than 700 offices country-wide.

ATM card The automatic teller machine card can be used both in Mexico and the U.S. with the STAR, PLUS and EXPLORE systems.

Direct deposit of retirement checks Retirement checks can be automatically deposited in your account.

For more information about the Friendship Senior Checking Account, contact California Commerce Bank, 811 Wilshire Blvd., Los Angeles, CA 90017, PO Box 30886, Los Angeles, CA. Tel: (213) 624-5700.

An easy way for holders of Mexican residency visas to transfer money from the U.S. to Mexico is through Wells Fargo's Inter-cuenta Express. This safe and fast method allows you to wire up to $1,000 per day to any Banamex Bank in Mexico. The money arrives the next day. To take advantage of this service, you must have a Banamex account. For more information, call Wells Fargo at 1-800-556-0605.

DEVALUATION

To help you understand how devaluation affects you financially, we'll give you a quick lesson in currency markets.

International money markets are driven by supply and demand, with speculators, national treasuries and businesses aggressively buying and selling daily. When a currency's value is fixed by the government, the time will come when it is no longer possible to keep trading it at high levels.

When speculators begin selling currencies on the open market, the government must step in and buy large quantities to keep its value up. When the government can no longer artificially maintain its currency's value through purchasing, it announces a devaluation.

That is exactly what Mexican President Ernesto Zedillo did in 1994, and then he went a step further. Due to growing investor concern over Mexico's growing, "dollar-linked" debt, Zedillo devalued the peso 15 percent. This devaluation triggered further pressures, and when the government allowed the peso to "float" freely on the international market, it's value fell 40 percent in one month.

In a system of floating exchange rates, this devastating crash would not have happened. The weak currency would have appreciated gradually.

It is important to understand how the devaluation of the peso will affect you and your business in Mexico. If your income is in dollars, which you periodically exchange into pesos to cover living and operating expenses, the peso devaluation is good for you. With each devaluation, your dollar attains more buying power. This is what makes Mexico so popular, especially for the retiree on a fixed income.

However, if you're earning in pesos or have investments valued in pesos, your portfolio could turn gloomy come devaluation. During the 1994 devaluation, these investments lost 40 percent of their value in less than a month!

That catastrophic loss, combined with rising inflation, will send your buying power into a downward spiral -- prices rise every day, and your daily income shrinks. Enough said?

Many expat investors protect themselves from Mexico's frequent currency devaluations by establishing business in which transactions are commonly carried out in dollars -- tourism or exporting, for example. Merchandise with values fixed in dollars will "increase" in value as the peso declines. But tourists and other clients accustomed to paying in dollars, won't even notice the price increase.

A $3.00 souvenir may cost six pesos prior to devaluation. Following a devaluation, however, its dollar price will remain the same, even though its peso price shoots up 40 or 50 percent. Pricing and selling in dollars is a safe way to hedge the devaluation gamble.

THE FINAL WORD

Mexico has a long history of abrupt and disruptive peso devaluations that roughly follow the country's political cycle. Entrepreneurs looking for opportunities in Mexico should consider that the peso has steadily increased in value all through 1997. The same behavior is expected in 1998. Given the current trends, the next major devaluation could happen in 2000.

The country is keeping its peso artificially high to lure foreign investment and keep inflation at bay. In doing so, Mexico is jeopardizing its competitiveness in the world market and harming its domestic economy. Be careful! The enticing exchange rate that lures you to Mexico could one day lead to financial ruin if you're not careful with you investments.

TAXES

If you're looking for an overseas haven where no taxes are charged on income, capital gains or wealth, Mexico is *not* the place to go. Mexicans are taxed for everything imaginable, but U.S. citizens and Canadians living abroad full or part time may be entitled to various deductions, exclusions and credits under national tax laws and international bilateral tax treaties.

We don't recommend that some eager entrepreneur heads to Mexico and establishes a business to try and beat the U.S. Internal Revenue Service through tax "avoidance." It's not worth it.

Time spent just getting your business off the ground, and *not* spent trying to find all the tax loopholes, will be well worth it.

But if you are looking to "get lost" abroad, you aren't alone. A 1985 IRS study revealed that of the 225,000 U.S. citizens presumed to be living in Mexico, only 4,800 filed tax returns. All those tax dodgers must see some advantage in Mexican life, but don't say we didn't warn you.

The Mexican tax system has undergone comprehensive reform to make it more competitive with those of Mexico's most important trading and investment partners and competitors.

PRINCIPAL TAXES

The major taxes payable by individuals and corporations operating in Mexico and, in certain cases, by foreign companies, are those levied by the federal government. State and municipal governments have more limited taxing powers.

Non-resident Corporations and Individuals The Income Tax Law contains specific rules for the taxation of Mexican-source income of non-resident corporations and individuals. Non-residents are only taxed on their Mexican-source income at rates that are applied separately to different types of gross income, with no deductions. No overall annual tax return is generally required of non-residents.

Branches of foreign corporations operating in Mexico are generally subject to the same tax rules as Mexican corporations. Most of the same compliance formalities and taxable income determinations apply. Certain home/office expenses are deductible, together with other expenses incurred in Mexico or abroad, even if determined on a pro-rata basis. No further tax is imposed on remittance of income that has been subject to the 34 percent federal corporate tax.

Resident Individuals Residents of Mexico, regardless of nationality, are subject to Mexican taxation on all types of worldwide income and must include this income on an annual personal income tax return. Special treatment is given to capital gains, domestic interest and dividend income. The tax rate schedule ranges from three to 35 percent. The table on the following page shows tax rates as of December 1997.

According to the Federal Tax Code, foreigners are considered residents of Mexico for tax purposes when they have established their home in Mexico, remain in the country for at least six months per year and cannot prove residence for tax purposes in another country.

Individuals with temporary or permanent immigration visas are usually considered residents, unless they spend less than six months in-country per year. Residents who spend more time out of Mexico than in, will only be taxed on their Mexican income.

Foreigners working in Mexico under a visitor's permit will probably not be considered residents for tax purposes until they

Taxable Income in Pesos*

Column 1 From	To	Basic Tax Tax on Column 1	Percentage on excess
0.01	2,518.62	0.00	3
2,518.63	21,376.92	75.54	10
21,376.93	37,567.92	1,961.28	17
37,567.93	43,671.24	4,713.90	25
43,671.25	52,286.16	6,239.58	32
52,288.17	105,453.96	8,996.40	33
105,453.97	166,210.02	26,541.66	34
166,210.03	and more	47,198.70	35

*Tax rates are updated every six months

establish some type of physical home in Mexico and remain in the country for at least six months per year.

REDUCING DOUBLE TAXATION

Many U.S. companies establish offices or factories in Mexico and then repatriate their profits back to the U.S. Unfortunately, this sometimes results in taxation in both countries. The U.S.-Mexico Tax Treaty, which went into effect Jan. 1, 1994, together with the North American Free Trade Agreement (NAFTA), greatly reduces the risk of double taxation.

Under the tax treaty, a U.S. resident (either an individual or legal entity) will be subject to Mexican taxes on its business income generated in Mexico if it has guaranteed such income through a permanent establishment in Mexico. The tax treaty specifically states that U.S. companies or individuals who obtain benefits under the tax treaty are in no way limited to claim available foreign tax credits in the United States for any taxes paid in Mexico.

Even with the reduced tax rates applied under the tax treaty, a U.S. company or individual entitled to receive a foreign tax credit will be able to credit Mexican taxes paid against its U.S. taxes due.

VALUE ADDED TAXES

A value-added tax (VAT) at the general rate of 15 percent is payable on the sale of goods, rendering of services, rents and importation of goods and services. In Free Zones, the tax is 10 percent.

CAPITAL GAINS TAX

Capital gains tax is based on 34 percent of the gain when selling or 20 percent of the sale price. Foreigners who have FM-2 or FM-3 residency status, who own real estate in Mexico and have lived two or more years in their Mexican home will not be charged capital gains tax when the Mexican home is sold. To avoid this tax, the expatriate must provide ample proof of two years' residency in Mexico including, phone bills, electricity or water bills and proof of FM-2 or FM-3 immigrant status.

TAX EXCEPTIONS FOR U.S. EXPATS

All U.S. citizens, no matter where in the world they live, are subject to the same tax laws as the neighbors they left behind in the U.S.

However, there are some important exceptions. The first is that the U.S. government grants a $70,000 exemption on earned income. To receive this exemption, you must be out of the States for 330 days in a 365-day period.

It is important to note that this is not a deduction, credit or deferral. *It is an outright tax exclusion for those who live outside the U.S.*

If you work overseas and maintain a place of residence in the United States, your tax home is not outside the United States. In other words, to qualify for the foreign-earned-income exclusion, you have to establish both your place of business and your residence outside the United States. *You need to sell or rent your U.S. home and establish a primary residence outside the United States.*

If you meet the following requirements, the U.S. Internal Revenue Service (IRS) will consider you a legitimate foreign resident who qualifies for the $70,000 exemption on earned income.

Local involvement: You should show involvement in local social and community activities to the same extent you were involved in such activities in the United States.

Personal belongings: The more you take to the foreign country, the more you are seen as establishing a foreign residence.

Local documents: It is helpful to obtain a foreign driver's license and foreign voter registration when possible.

Sleeping quarters: A transient is more likely to sleep in a hotel; a resident likely owns housing or signs at least a year-long lease.

U.S. property: Owning a vacant U.S. residence is a sign of an intention not to establish a foreign residence. You must sell or rent your U.S. residence to qualify.

Foreign taxes: This is the most important consideration for anyone trying to qualify for the foreign-earned-income exclusion. Foreign countries tax on the basis of residence. If you claim exemption from local taxes because you are not a resident of that country, the IRS will conclude that you are a U.S. resident and do not qualify for the foreign-earned-income exclusion under the foreign-residence test.

The $70,000 limit applies to individual single taxpayers. If you are married, you and your spouse potentially can exclude up to $140,000 of foreign-earned income. But you cannot share each other's limit. For example, if one of you earns $85,000 and the other earns $35,000, you exclude only $105,000 on the return ($70,000 plus $35,000).

Remember, to get the exemption *you must file a tax return and claim the exemption on Form 2555.* The IRS has had success in recent years contending that anyone who does not file a tax return loses the benefit, even if he or she meets all the other requirements.

This exemption does not apply to dividends, pensions and other similar forms of earnings. U.S. residents here have loudly complained about being taxed on their pensions.

If you pay taxes to a foreign country, those taxes can be exempted from your U.S. taxes.

Even if you receive no income in Mexico, it is still very important to file the standard tax form 1040. If you live here for a number of years and then decide to return to the United States, it looks highly suspicious if you haven't filed a return in a long time.

THE FINAL WORD

Foreign business owners may be targets for special scrutiny by Mexican tax collectors. Many Mexicans don't follow the correct tax procedures, but that is no reason why foreign residents should follow suit. We strongly recommend that foreign business owners play by the rules.

U.S. citizens need to remember that their $70,000 exemption is on earned income and not on profits from capital gains or other business investments. Be sure you hire a tax accountant specializing in overseas incomes who can assist you in taking advantage of all the benefits and deductions you have coming.

MEXICO ON THE INTERNET

Information Age — The modern era when computers and technology enable quick access to data from anywhere in the world at any time.

Cyber Space is fast becoming an indispensable tool for the entrepreneur and retiree living abroad. Expats with a personal computer and access to the Internet can now live and do business even in the smallest, most isolated town in Mexico.

In the past, without the use of new technology like e-mail or Internetphone or the World Wide Web, living abroad was inconvenient and costly.

But now, individuals of small businesses, such as mail order companies, import/export firms or bed and breakfasts can establish themselves anywhere and create a worldwide presence by having a "store front" on the Internet, selling their products and services.

Mary Bragg, owner of Pancho's Restaurant in Cabo San Lucas, doesn't even have a web page but thanks the Internet for 40 to 50 percent of her customers. She simply asks her customers to mention Pancho's while surfing the web. That's all it took for diners to begin arriving at her restaurant with a computer print out in hand saying, "Go to Pancho's, it's the best in Cabo."

Cybercommerce Sellers located in remote towns can use

their Mexican or international Visa or Mastercard Electronic Merchant Bankcard Service to accept and deposit money from sales in other parts of the world directly into their Mexican or international bank accounts. And as "cybercommerce," or business transacting over the Internet, prospers, we will soon see the creation of a new digital or "cyber money" to help merchants deal with troublesome currency conversions or devaluations.

Cyber Research The Internet puts vital information on laws affecting foreigners, trends in business, important contacts and current exchange rates only a mouse click away — no matter where in the world you decide to live and work.

Hundreds of web sites can help make your transition to Mexican life easier. Wondering how to handle your banking matters in Mexico? Simply access the Lloyds investment page at www.mexconnect.com/MEX/lloyds/llydeco9.html to learn about their special investment programs for foreigners. Considering retirement life in Mazatlán? "Surf" the net for names of real estate agents and review the schedules for retirement seminars focused on this resort community at wwww.maztravel.com

Discussion groups, which enable you to get sometimes instantaneous answers, make the Internet the ultimate networking tool. It's easy to use the net to hook up with groups of retirees or businesspeople with similar interests. Try www.livingoverseas.com (that's ours) or www.mexconnect.com. These news groups enable researchers to pose questions to thousands of people at once; one of them is bound to have the information you seek. By subscribing to a "chat board," you can conduct a simultaneous "conversation" with people all over the world through your computer and modem — how's that for networking?

MEXICO ON-LINE

The Internet has been growing 20 to 30 percent per month in Mexico, but is still in its infant stage. Some 150 Internet service providers (ISPs) serve less than 100,000 dial-up customers. Larger ISPs include Telmex, Infosel, Internet de Mexico and CompuServe. The average cost to go on-line is only around $20 a month.

Computerless researchers can go to one of the "cyber cafés" that are springing up in cities and towns throughout Mexico. These cafés provide public computer terminals with access to the net — and they offer a great cup of coffee. The cyber café can set you up with your own e-mail account to send and receive messages for as little as $3.00 to $4.00 per hour.

PUTTING THE INTERNET TO WORK

The Internet was born in the late 1960s, when the U.S. Department of Defense set out to develop a network that tied together geographically distant computers using a technology of sharing data lines called "packet-switching."

What they came up with was a series of computers connected together that spoke the same networking language. Add hundreds of thousands of computers to that first, humble network and the Internet of today takes form. Creative entrepreneurs have discovered how to save big money putting the Internet to work for them.

E-mail is the most valuable Internet resource for small international companies. It enables cheap, instantaneous, written communication with anyone in the world who also has Internet access. A 10-minute telephone call to New York from your beach home in Cozumel, Mexico, could cost $30 or more. But if you correspond with your colleague in New York — or anywhere else in the world — via e-mail, you are charged only the price of a quick, local call to your Internet provider to log on and send your message. See what we mean?

The World Wide Web, often called the "WWW" or simply "the web," is a collection of millions of "home pages" dedicated to topics on every subject under the sun. The web stands out among earlier generations of technology in that it provides sound, text, and pictures in an easy-to-use format.

Expats use the web to research business ideas and look for contacts, as well as market their own products and services, keep updated with world news and have fun.

Internet Service Providers (ISPs) are organizations or companies, big and small, that provide Internet service or access to their subscribers. They're the ones who give you the numbers that your modem calls to access and surf the net. You can think of an ISP as your "on and off-ramp" to the Internet.

Internet telephone is not being used much by expats in Mexico, because the quality is still far below that of a regular telephone call.

Calling over the net is dirt cheap, but transmission delays and sound quality make it more like talking on a ham or a two-way radio than on an honest-to-goodness telephone. Using software such as Internetphone, sold in computer stores everywhere, people with Internet access can call each other over the Internet and save big money. Internetphone users may only call other Internetphone users, and only providing the receiver's computer is on-line at the time of the call. Special cameras can also be purchased that enable Internetphone callers to see each other as they talk, via the computer screens. Both must have these little cameras, of course.

Another software package, Net2phone, enables people with Internet access to call any *regular* telephone, also at big savings over regular, long-distance rates.

Quality still leaves much to be desired, with three to five second delays in transmission time and poorer sound, but this technology enables you to save a small fortune on long distance phone bills, and quality is improving all the time.

Videoconferencing, using similar technology as Internetphone with camera, will be the communication tool of choice for overseas entrepreneurs and retirees as soon as all the kinks are worked out.

Face to face communications without the cost and inconveniences of overseas travel is an expat's dream. We've heard of business owners planning to install cameras in their stores and offices, so they can keep visual tabs on their Mexican operation, even from abroad.

One popular videoconferencing software program, Cu-SeeMe, retails for only $99 and can be down-loaded on a trial basis over the Internet (www.wpine.com). Videoconferencing companies are working fast to improve visual and sound clarity and simplify set up. Currently, a videoconference requires a video-capture board, a video camera, a modem and videoconferencing software — too complicated for most micro entrepreneurs, us included!

WEB SITES

On-line international computer services makes researching your Latin American investment as easy as switching on a modem and clicking a mouse. A wealth of information about Mexico and South America is available on "the net," and opportunities exist for those adept at computerized searches.

We've compiled a list of important search services and web pages to help you get started. Within these web pages you'll find hundreds of other "links" to related information on other sites that could also be helpful. The Internet is now an indispensable research tool for everything from replacement computer parts to valuable overseas contacts. If your not on-line now, you better hurry up and get on!

Mexico Online This electronic bulletin board system permits computer users to obtain up-to-the-minute information about traveling, retirement or doing business in Mexico. http://www.mexonline.com

MEXIS On-Line Date Services provides access to international e-mail, legal information, books, magazines, NAFTA text, financial reports on Mexican companies, articles, research reports and the Diario Oficial. Mexico Information Services, PO Box 11770 Fort Worth, TX 76110; Tel: (817) 924-0746; U.S. only (800) 446-0746; Fax: (817) 924-9687

MexNET On-Line provides on-line access to trade leads, e-mail, communications with Mexican companies, NAFTA schedules, regulations, event calendar, business card directory and classified advertisements. U.S. Office: 2810 South 400 West, Salt Lake City, UT 84115. Tel: (801) 486-8181; Fax (801) 486-6969. Mexico Office: Calz. de Tlalpan 2250, Col Avante, 04460 Mexico, D.F.; Tel: (5) 549-9267; Fax: (5) 544-7724.

The Latin American Network Information Center (LANIC) is the home page of the University of Texas' Center for Latin American Studies. LANIC contains everything from documents produced by the Latin American and Caribbean Center at Florida International University, to regional maps and electronic books about the region. Also available on LANIC is the New

Mexico State University Library "Guide to Internet Resources for Latin America." http://lanic.utexas.edu/

Simpex Information includes import/export regulations and financing options as well as other data base information. http://mexico.businessline.gob.mx

Living Abroad Magazine has useful information for overseas executives. http://www.livingabroad.com

Foreign Exchange Rates Up-to-date exchange rates on the peso or any international currency. http://www.bloomberg.com/markets/currency.html

Offshore Tax Havens Good site for information about tax havens around the world. http://www.cadvision.com/nolimits/offshore.html

Mexico Living and Business Site Good, fun page on just about everything to do with living and doing business in Mexico. http://www.mexweb.com

NAFTA Home Page Straight from the U.S. Department of Commerce. http://iepnt1.itaiep.doc.gov/nafts 2 htm

U.S. Commercial Service of Mexico Maintained by the office of the U.S. Foreign Commercial Service at the American Embassy of Mexico City. http://www.uscommerce.org.mx

Mexico Business Home Page Sample articles from this popular monthly magazine. http://www.nafta.net/mexbiz/index.html

U.S. Department of Commerce - Mexico Many resources and reports to help you understand business in Mexico. http://www.stat-usa.gov/bems/bemsmex/bemsmex.html

Lloyd's Investments Lloyd's is a popular investment consultant in Mexico and cashes residents' North American checks. http://www.mexconnect.com/mex/lloyds/llyclesco9.html

Mexico General information on everything Mexican. http://www.mexconnect.com

Lonely Planet Books Good site to gather travel info on Mexico. http://www.lonelyplanet.com

U.S./Mexico Business A great on-line version and more of the monthly business magazine. http://www.mexicobusiness.com

Ministry of Tourism The official site for this important Mexican ministry. http://www.mexico-travel.com

Mexico-Related Links Link up with currency exchange, FAQ, politicial commentaries and language schools in Mexico and more. http://www.eden.com/~tomzap/links.html

Travel Mexico Planning a trip to Mexico? Check this site out. http://www.wotw.com/wow/mexico/mexico.html

Cancún Online Everything about the most popular travel destination in Mexico. http://www.cancun.com

WEB SITES FOR JOB HUNTERS

www.overseasjobs.com Comprehensive site that offers job search capabilities as well as links to other relevant sites.

www.state.gov. U.S. State Dept. Offers 1,000 internships annually; complete information and application on home page.

www.transabroad.com Transitions Abroad's website contains an on-line database that serves as a complete guide to working, living and learning overseas. This searchable database is a compilation of articles and resource directories published in Transitions' bimonthly magazine. You can order any of their publications online.

HOTEL AND PLANE RESERVATIONS

http://www.flifo.com   http://www.travelocity.com
http://www.itn.net   http://www.previewtravel.com/index.html

Artisans like Luis Rodríguez are beginning to realize how modern computer and telecommunications technology can increase their sales tenfold. Luis sells his beautiful, hand-made pottery to exporters for only $1.50 each. The same pieces fetch $25.00 or more farther north.

RESIDENCY

In the past, most foreigners who settled in Mexico were retirees seeking to live well and economically on their fixed social security income, or executives sent by large, multinational companies.

But expatriate demographics are changing. Today, most newcomers to Mexico are sent by small companies to set up offshore offices or are simply energetic entrepreneurs looking for business opportunities with low start-up costs.

Our own informal study reveals the most common reasons why North Americans move to Mexico:

Company transfers them   Tired of high taxes
Get more for their money   Learn a second language
New business opportunities   Seeking adventure
Stretch the pension   Escape from high crime
Escape the cold weather   Spiritual renewal
Tired of the rat race   Escape government intrusion
College grads fleeing corporate America

Before the North American Free Trade Agreement (NAFTA) went into effect, retirees were the only group that could easily obtain a resident status. Business people and entrepreneurs found it practically impossible.

Today, NAFTA has made it easier for the foreign business community to reside in Mexico. The FM-2 and FM-3 temporary residency visas are now readily available for retirees and future business owners.

Mexico's immigration laws provide for many types of foreign residency, depending on whether the in-country stay is for business, hourly work or retirement. All visas are issued by the Ministry of the Interior (*Secretaría de Gobernación*).

The process to acquire anything but a temporary tourist visa can be time-consuming and bureaucratic, but like most Mexican procedures, loopholes and shortcuts exist to help skirt the bureaucratic mire. With good contacts and a little innovation, you can accomplish just about anything in Mexico.

You can apply for residency yourself, and many local expats will tell you how. Nonetheless, we feel your time is better spent planning your money-making activities rather than standing in line and dealing with Mexican bureaucracy.

TIPS *Contact "Mago" at her office in Lake Chapala for honest, inexpensive assistance in acquiring your residency visa. True to her name, Mago is a "magician" at wading through bureaucracy. She began working out of the back of her flower shop, helping foreigners get their FM-3-2 residency visas. She now has an office next to the shop, and charges around $200 for retirement visas and $500 for business visas. Contact Mago in Mexico at Tel: 376-5-4199.*

Many U.S. or Canadian citizens who take up temporary or permanent residency in Mexico worry how this will effect their citizenship back home -- especially today, as more and more North Americans renounce their own citizenship to live abroad.

One high-profile case was that of Kenneth Dart, the billionaire foam cup maker who renounced his U.S. citizenship and went to live in the Central American nation of Belize to save millions per year he was paying in U.S. taxes.

In special cases like this, these mostly wealthy U.S. citizens *voluntarily* gave up their U.S. citizenship. Temporary or permanent residency abroad will not, in any way, jeopardize your U.S. or Canadian citizenship. Don't worry!

TOURIST VISA (FM-T)

Foreigners can easily enter Mexico by means of the readily available tourist card (FM-T). These cards are issued free-of-charge at Mexican immigration border checkpoints, as well as at all international airports and seaports. To obtain the card, Mexican officials will require proof of citizenship from your home country, such as a passport, birth certificate or voter registration card, plus a photo identification, such as a driver's license. The card is valid for six months. No proof of income is required.

FM-T holders must leave Mexico before their six-month visa expires. If they arrived by car or other vehicle with foreign license plates, they must leave in that vehicle as well.

The majority of foreigners live in Mexico on a tourist visa. Many have lived in Mexico for years without ever encountering problems due to their resident status. Holders of the FM-T tourist card are not permitted to work in Mexico for wages. Artists and writers may work in-country, as long as they export the work they sell.

If you're planning to live in Mexico only part of the year, you could probably get by with just a tourist card. However, people with only tourist status (FM-T) are prohibited from importing household furnishings and other comforts from their home country, as well as opening a Mexican checking or savings account and obtaining a Mexican driver's license.

If you plan to live in Mexico more than six months per year, or if you plan to work full or part time, you should consider applying for a permanent FM-2 or FM-3 immigrant status.

TEMPORARY, NON-IMMIGRANT STATUS (FM-3)

The FM-3 visa is the residency option for students, paid and non-paid visitors, business people, investors, commercial representatives, technicians, scientists, retirees, professionals, staff aids, artists, athletes, cultural ministers or family members of any of the previously mentioned. This is a temporary

Mago is famous in the Lake Chapala area for her ability to cut through the red tape to acquire everything from residency visas for foreign residents to hard-to-get telephone lines. Look her up!

residency status that is granted for a one-year period and is renewable for up to five years. FM-3 status is relatively easy to obtain, providing all the paperwork is in order. The application fee and yearly renewal fee are both around $80.00. Some FM-3 status benefits include:

❀Avoidance of capital gains tax on a home inhabited for at least two years prior to its sale.
❀The right to bring a vehicle with foreign plates into Mexico without any time restrictions.
❀The right to import used household furnishings and personal belongings.
❀The right to apply for a Mexican driver's license.
❀Those who own Mexican homes only need to prove 50 percent of the minimum salary requirements to obtain and maintain this residency status.
❀The right to obtain a Mexican checking and savings account.

Benefits vary depending on the type of FM-3 visa held. This status may also cover a dependent spouse or family members.

Those applying for the FM-3 pensioner visa (following number VIII) must have a monthly income outside of Mexico. A pensioner is a person who lives on his/her own financial resources generated outside Mexico through investments in capital stocks, bonds, national credit institutions, pensions or other compensation recognized by the Mexican Immigration Office.

To determine a pensioner's minimum required monthly income, the government uses a formula based on the minimum daily salary earned by a Mexican worker in Mexico City (*Distrito Federal*), multiplied by a set number of days.

Example: At press time the daily Mexican wage was $26.50 pesos. Applicants applying for FM-3 pensioner visas are required to demonstrate a monthly income based on 250 days x $26.50 pesos, or $6,225 pesos monthly (U.S. $828).

For a spouse and each dependent child, the FM-3 pensioner must show an additional $414 monthly (125 days x $26.50 pesos = $3,312 pesos or U.S. $414).

The FM-3 visa can be issued under the following classifications:

I. Student
Validity: One day to 12 months with annual extension

Students are individuals who come into the country to study in state or private institutions. The student is required to present proof of acceptance in the school. This acceptance must be signed by the school director and be on school letterhead. Annual extension can be obtained. Students may remain in Mexico for the duration of their studies or long enough to obtain their final documentation from the school. They cannot be outside of Mexico for more than 120 days per year. In order to maintain their student status, students must register at the National Foreign Registry (*Registro Nacional de Extranjeros*).

Temporary importation of vehicle Same requirements as tourists. Car permit will be extended every year, as long as the FM-3 is renewed before it expires.

II. Visitor Not Remunerated
Validity: One day to 12 months

This visa is for individuals who are not engaged in remunerative or lucrative activities. It is an option for tourists who wish to remain in Mexico more than six months. Annual extension must be obtained. Household furnishings cannot be brought into Mexico under this category.

Temporary importation of vehicle Same requirements as tourists. Car permit will be extended every year, as long as the FM-3 is renewed before it expires.

III. Visitor Remunerated (Small business owners)
Validity: One day to 12 months

This visa is for visitors engaged in remunerative or lucrative activities. It is for people engaged in independent activities other than those listed here. In this as well as in the next FM-3 categories, your future employer should issue an acceptance letter indicating the position you're going to hold. *If you will be self-employed, issue the letter yourself.* Annual extension must be obtained. Household effects can be brought into Mexico under this category. See Owning a Business for more details.

Temporary importation of a vehicle A car permit will be extended every year, as long as the FM-3 is renewed before it expires.

IV. Business
Validity: One day to 12 months

Under the business visa, a person can come to the country to attend meetings of administrative boards of enterprises or to make business deals. This business visa applies only to foreigners not included in the NAFTA treaty, or North American business people wishing to remain in Mexico for business for more than 30 days. Annual extension must be obtained. Household effects cannot be brought into Mexico under this category.

Temporary importation of a vehicle Same requirements as tourists. Car permit will be extended every year, as long as the FM-3 is renewed before it expires.

V. Investors
Validity: 12 months

An investor is someone who invests his or her capital in any type of industry according to national laws. Such an investment should contribute to the economic and social development of Mexico. If the investment is at least 26,000 times the minimum wage in the Federal District (Mexico City), a document available at the National Registry of Foreign Investments should be presented to the Mexican Immigration Office. Annual extension must be obtained. Household effects can be brought into Mexico under this category.

Temporary importation of vehicle Same requirements as tourists. Car permit will be extended every year, as long as the FM-3 is renewed before it expires.

VI. Commercial Representative
Validity: 12 months

A commercial representative is a person transferred from the U.S. or Canada to represent a U.S. or Canadian company in

Mexico. Annual extension must be obtained. Household effects can be brought into Mexico under this category.

Temporary importation of vehicle Same requirements as tourists. Car permit will be extended every year, as long as the FM-3 is renewed before it expires.

VII. Technicians and Scientists
Validity: 12 months

Technicians perform technical investigations within the country. When they apply for a visa, they should indicate the type of project or activity they are involved in. To obtain this visa, the applicant must show that the function cannot be carried out by a Mexican citizen.

Scientists conduct or perform scientific investigations. An applicant must prove that he/she is highly skilled in his/her area and that the work will contribute to the development of science and technology in Mexico. Annual extension must be obtained. Household effects can be brought into Mexico under this category.

Temporary importation of vehicle Same requirements as tourists. Car permit will be extended every year, as long as the FM-3 is renewed before it expires.

VIII. Pensioner or Rentista
Validity: 12 months

A pensioner is a person who lives on his/her own financial resources generated outside Mexico by investments of capital in stocks, bonds, national credit institutions or other organizations recognized by the Mexican Immigration Office. Current published income requirements for pensioners are 250 times the minimum salary in the Federal District (Mexico City), plus 125 times the minimum salary in the Federal District for each dependent.

Annual extension must be obtained. Household effects can be brought into Mexico under this category. The applicant must be older than 45 years.

Temporary importation of vehicle Same requirements as

tourists. Car permit will be extended every year, as long as the FM-3 is renewed before it expires.

IX. Professional
Validity: 12 months

Some occupations require government registration. If your occupation is approved by the Mexican government, you are required to register yourself at the Ministry of Education, from which you will obtain an official document allowing you to practice and reside in Mexico. Annual extension must be obtained. Household effects can be brought into Mexico under this category.

Temporary importation of vehicle Same requirements as tourists. Car permit will be extended every year, as long as the FM-3 is renewed before it expires.

X. Staff Aide
Validity: 12 months

A staff aide visa is granted to someone who occupies a position in a trust or administrative firm or institution located in Mexico. This visa will only be granted to people who occupy a unique position; a job done by no one else in the firm. The occupant of this position must present a certain standard of service according to the job. If the standard is reached, the FM-3 visa is obtained. Annual extension must be obtained. Household effects can be brought into Mexico under this category.

Temporary importation of vehicle Same requirements as tourists. Car permit will be extended every year, as long as the FM-3 is renewed before it expires.

XI. Relative
Validity: 12 months

A relative is a person who lives under the financial sponsorship of a spouse or an immediate relative with immigrant status or Mexican citizenship. Children, brothers and sisters of the petitioner may be admitted as dependents under the same migratory status as their sponsor. However, these people must be one of the following: a minor, a physically handicapped person who is unable to work, or a full-time student. Household effects cannot be brought into Mexico under this category.

Temporary importation of vehicle A foreign vehicle cannot be brought into Mexico under this category.

XII. Artist and Athlete
Validity: 12 months

This category requires an acceptance letter from the employer in Mexico and a certificate from the union, association or federation to which the artist or athlete belongs. Household effects can be brought into Mexico under this category.

Temporary importation of vehicle Same requirements as tourists. Car permit will be extended every year, as long as the FM-3 is renewed before it expires.

XIII. Cult Minister
Validity: 12 months

The religious association to which the applicant belongs must request the FM-3 visa. In this letter, the association must indicate the area in which the applicant will preach or serve as missionary.

Temporary importation of vehicle Same requirements as tourists. Car permit will be extended every year, as long as the FM-3 is renewed before it expires.

XIV. Distinguished Visitor FM-16
Validity: 12 months

A distinguished visitor requires international recognition in his/her field. An educational, scientific or artistic institution or even a public or private press agency must indicate the reason for the visit.

XV. NAFTA visa FMN
Validity: 30 days

A Canadian or U.S. citizen seeking to engage in business activities in Mexico has a right to this visa under the North American Free Trade Agreement (NAFTA). However, this person cannot receive remuneration for his/her business activities while in Mexico.

Temporary importation of vehicle A foreign vehicle cannot be brought into Mexico under this category.

How to Apply for FM-3 Status The following documents are required to obtain an FM-3 visa:

❁An application letter. The Migratory Services Office will prepare this letter for you free-of-charge.

❁A reference letter in Spanish signed by two people who state they know the applicant and can testify to the applicant's domicile. A form letter created for this purpose is available in the same office.

❁A photo copy of the applicant's passport notarized by a Mexican notary public, plus the original and two copies of the applicant's FM-T tourist visa.

❁Proof of income. Applicants who receive social security or other government benefits can obtain letters certifying this income from the nearest U.S. embassy or consulate. Proof must be provided that the last three of these monthly payments were deposited in a Mexican bank.

If additional income comes from a Mexican or foreign bank, the applicant must present notarized letters, translated into Spanish, from each institution certifying the monthly amount received, along with a copy of the certificate of deposit or other instrument.

❁Married couple applicants must submit a translated and certified copy of their marriage certificate.

TRANSLATION OF DOCUMENTS

Any document originating in a foreign country must be officially translated into Spanish. If the document is not issued from an official government agency, it must also be authenticated by a notary public in its country of origin. Such documents include bank letters that serve as proof of income.

All translations must be done by an official translator who is recognized by the Mexican Judicial System. Contact the nearest

Mexican Embassy for information about translating services and their respective fees.

All other documents must be certified by the Mexican consulate or embassy closest to the document's place of origin. For example, a marriage certificate issued in Los Angeles, California, must be certified in Los Angeles. If the same person was born in Texas, however, his or her birth certificate must be certified by the Mexican consul in Texas.

Any document notarized by a Mexican embassy or consulate in a foreign country must also be notarized by a Mexican, in-country notary public.

IMMIGRANT STATUS FM-2

The FM-2 visa is considered an introductory phase prior to becoming a permanent resident. After five years as an FM-2 resident, a foreigner may become a permanent resident of Mexico.

The requirements of the FM-2 status are more demanding than those of the FM-3. The FM-2 status was once necessary to own property in Mexico. But with the establishment of the 1993 Foreign Investment Law, which enables foreigners to own property outright, this status isn't as sought-after as it used to be.

The holder of this visa must renew each year by resubmitting proof of income and paying the required $160 fee. The FM-2 visa holder must remain in Mexico at least 180 days per year. However, if the holder remains outside of Mexico more than 18 months during the five-year period, permanent residency will not be granted.

FM-2 visa holders who remain outside of Mexico for more than two years will lose their status. Those who are outside Mexico when their visa expires can reapply within 30 days of the expiration date. They must prove that they were out of the country. FM-2 residents must spend one entire day in Mexico between each exit.

Holders of this status enjoy all the benefits of the FM-3 visa holder, such as the exemption from capital gains tax and a 50 percent monthly income reduction if the resident owns his or her Mexican home. The FM-2 visa can be issued under the following classifications:

I. Rentista

Applicant must have a monthly income equal or greater to 400 times the minimum wage earned by a Mexican worker in Mexico City (calculated the same as the FM-3). Also required is a letter from a bank proving that the applicant will have the required income for at least one year, or six months if the applicant owns a home in Mexico.

II. Administration

Company officials may obtain an FM-2 visa, but only if they can prove they are uniquely qualified for the position.

III. Investor

Anyone who invests the equivalent of 40,000 days times the minimum wage of a Mexican worker in Mexico City can receive FM-2 residency status.

IV. Professionals, Technicians and Scientists

In exceptional cases, a professional visa may be granted to outstanding experts or specialized professors. Performing arts and athletes are now eligible for FM-3 status.

V. Family Dependents

Dependents of an FM-2 visa holder who are a spouse or second-degree blood relative are eligible for non-work visas.

Foreigners married to Mexicans or with Mexican-born children may apply for FM-2 status by including with the residency application letter a marriage certificate and evidence of sufficient economic resources to maintain a family. Under this classification, foreigners may work in Mexico with the approval of the Ministry of the Interior.

PERMANENT RESIDENCY (INMIGRADO)

Once an FM-2 visa holder has lived in Mexico for five years, he or she is eligible to become a permanent resident or inmigrado. The permanent status is not automatic, rather it is subject to the discretion of the Ministry of the Interior. The permanent resident or inmigrado enjoys all the rights of a Mexican citizen, except the privilege of voting in political elections. The advantage of obtaining an inmigrado status is the opportunity to work in Mexico with few restrictions.

If the applicant owns a car with foreign license plates, the car must be removed from the country before *inmigrado* status will be granted. A permanent resident may only own vehicles with Mexican plates.

How to Apply for FM-2 Status The application procedure to acquire FM-2 resident status is the same as to acquire FM-3 migratory status. In addition, the applicant must submit an official birth certificate with the official seal of the county or state issuing agent. The certificate must be translated and authenticated just as any document described in the application and translation procedures for the FM-3 status.

If the FM-2 status is approved, the applicant's fingerprints will be taken before the residency booklet is issued. Also required are 13 black and white, four centimeter by four centimeter photographs — eight front photos and five profiles of the right side of the face, showing forehead and ears, without glasses, earrings or hair covering the face or ears.

Application procedures and requirements for both the FM-2 and FM-3 residency visas change frequently. Contact the Immigration Office in Mexico City or Guadalajara for up-to-date information about required documentation and procedures.

THE FINAL WORD

When you're ready to apply for your residency visa, ask around in the popular expat communities for a reliable person who can process it for you quickly and economically. Attorneys can charge $1,000 or more, while experienced "residency processors" can do the same job for around $200. Or, if you speak Spanish well, you can do it yourself for free.

You don't have to be an attorney to process residency applications, so why pay more?

MOVING FURNITURE

The U.S. and Mexico are opening their doors to each other's freight companies, which should benefit the foreigner wanting to transfer household goods and other merchandise across the border.

Prior to NAFTA, U.S. trucks had to drop their trailers at the Mexican border, handing-off their loads to a Mexican counterpart. Today, North American moving companies can carry international cargo to Mexican states contiguous to the United States. By 2000, they will have "cross-border" access to all of Mexico.

But problems still exist. U.S. freight forwarders cite border delays as the number one problem when moving cargo to Mexico. The monopoly still enjoyed by Mexican freight brokers to clear cargo through customs is to blame for the slow-down.

The Mexican government clamped down on widespread misappropriation and "disappearance" of customs duties and taxes by requiring that all freight stop on the U.S. side of the border until documents have been cleared and taxes paid. The procedure requires that U.S. trucks entrust their loads to a U.S. freight forwarder that is either owned or controlled by a Mexican broker. The days of delay caused by this extra bureaucratic step continues to keep speed-conscious shippers grumbling.

In spite of the bureaucracy, Mexican moving companies are working hard to provide more professional service, knowing that NAFTA will heat-up the competition.

REQUIREMENTS

Foreigners must obtain FM-2 or FM-3 resident status to move household furnishings and personal items duty-free to Mexico (see the Residency section for more information). The tourist visa does not permit importation of household goods.

Mexican law permits each FM-2 or FM-3 visa holder to import used "furniture and household items that are commonly found in an average Mexican family home." This could be very restrictive, since the average Mexican family only owns one television set, no clothes dryers and certainly not many of the luxury items that North Americans take for granted. Fortunately, the law isn't strictly enforced, and customs officials are accustomed to North American luxury items. They do set a strict limit, however, on the overall quantity of goods — only one household of articles may be imported by one family.

Articles that are six-months old or newer will be taxed at approximately 38 percent. The import of alcohol, including wine, firearms and illegal drugs is strictly forbidden.

COST AND PROCEDURES

According to Alex Beltrán at CIME, a Mexican-based moving company, it costs between $4,000 and $6,000 to move a three-bedroom home with approximately 5,000 lbs. of furnishings from California to Mexico City, insurance and tax included.

To begin processing your move, first obtain a FM-2 or FM-3 resident visa. Next, make a list in Spanish of all the items you'll be shipping and submit it to the nearest Mexican Consulate. It is not necessary to include each item's estimated value. It is advisable, however, to submit a separate list that includes all the articles approximate values to the moving company. This second list will be important for the purchase of moving insurance later on.

The Mexican Consulate will ask for copies of your passport and visa, and your current and future address in Mexico. They will then ask you to fill out other official forms that could change from consulate to consulate.

After all the official paperwork has been completed, the same Mexican Consulate will authorize your list of articles with an official stamp. The moving company contracted in the U.S. will be required to present photocopies of all documents to Mexican officials at the border.

CUSTOMS INSPECTION ROULETTE

Article inspections at the border are determined totally at random by a red or green light that illuminates when your transporation driver pushes a button. If the red light comes on, you lose! All your household furnishings will be unloaded and inspected at the border, causing at least a several hour delay. If the green light comes on, you may cross into your new, adopted land relatively unscathed. Good luck!

ADDITIONAL CONSIDERATIONS

It's a good idea to allow 10 to 14 days for a complete, California-to-Mexico City move. This is taking for granted that no major problems occur at the border.

Your itemized list of household furnishings and their values will help you acquire the proper amount of home owners insurance once you're established.

All FM-3 visa holders who decide to move back to their country of origin, are required by Mexican law to ship all their personal articles and furnishings out of the country. It is illegal to leave them behind or even sell them in Mexico. FM-2 residents, on the other hand, are permitted to sell their possessions or leave them behind.

THE FINAL WORD

Do-it-yourself furniture-moving to Mexico is a real headache. We recommend you hire a moving company with ample, across-the-border experience. The extra money you pay will be well worth it for your own peace of mind.

Most people only ship electronic equipment, such as computer, fax or stereo. Top quality, low cost home furnishings are sold in Mexico and can be acquired for little more than what you would pay hauling your old furnishings down.

DRIVING & INSURANCE

One of the biggest advantages of Mexico's proximity to the rest of North America is the ease and minimal expense with which foreign residents can bring their own car into the country. In more distant countries, foreigners are often required to pay outrageous import duties on their vehicle, even after paying considerable shipping fees.

With few exceptions, Mexican law permits foreigners with tourist visas or temporary or permanent visa status to drive and own a car with either Mexican or foreign license plates. A foreign-plated car may remain in Mexico as long as its owner's immigration documents are valid.

Mexican Plates Many permanent residents feel driving a Mexican-plated car helps them "fit in" better with their new surroundings and not stand out as tourists. Cars manufactured in Mexico include Chevrolets, Toyotas, Fords and Volkswagens. They are reasonably priced, but standards and quality are not as high as in the U.S.

The only disadvantage to owning a Mexican-plated car is the 3 to 5 percent yearly tax charged on the vehicle's value during your first 10 years of ownership.

Import Duties New cars brought into Mexico are charged high import duties, while used vehicles manufactured abroad cost 20 to 50 percent more.

Auto insurance is not required by Mexican law but should be a serious consideration for anyone driving in-country. Mexican police are authorized to arrest any uninsured driver involved in an accident, at least until fault is determined and reimbursement payments made.

A Mexican insurance policy is recognized by the authorities as a guarantee of payment for damages incurred. Presentation of the policy will speed early release.

NOTE: Beginning in 1998, insurance will be compulsory in the Mexican state of Jalisco. The proposed law requires motorists to insure themselves for at least $90,000 pesos ($11,250 U.S.) damage.

U.S. insurance is not valid in Mexico, but a Mexican policy can easily be purchased in border towns or at one of the many agencies throughout the country. All drivers should carry property and bodily injury coverage. Depending on the value of the car, liability coverage may also be desired. The annual premium

A brand new Volkswagen Beetle, manufactured in Mexico, sells for only $6,000

on a vehicle worth $10,000 with full coverage should run around $600. Insurance awards are usually limited to actual damages, so it doesn't pay to over insure.

For additional information on insuring your auto, contact *Sucesores* De Allen W. Lloyd, Insurance Agency. They have assisted foreigners for years and have offices throughout Mexico. In Guadalajara call (3) 121-9050. Or call Sanborns, another reputable company based in the U.S. at (800) 222-0158.

Foreign-plated cars may only be driven by the person to whom the car is registered. Permitting another person to drive the car may result in the vehicle's confiscation and a heavy fine. In 1997, this law was amended, and now FM-3 visa holders may now permit anyone to drive their car, as long as the visa holder goes along for the ride. Dependents can also drive the owners car.

PROCEDURES

The following explains the procedure for bringing a vehicle into Mexico. The procedures apply to all except those foreigners traveling only within 15 miles of a border, in Baja California or in the Sonora border region.

To import a vehicle into Mexico three forms must be completed at the border: The Temporary Vehicle Import Permit, the Vehicle Return Promise and the Tourist Entry Form.

The preceding forms may only be completed by including the original and one copy of the vehicle's title, registration and license receipt; a valid drivers license and the driver's birth certificate, passport or resident card. Leased or rented vehicles can only enter Mexico with the written authorization of their registered owners.

Government regulations require the driver post a bond to ensure the vehicle's return to its country of origin. The bond may be posted with a credit card, a vehicle-value bond or a cash deposit. The surcharge for credit card deposits is $11.00.

BOND PROCEDURE

Drivers who have already submitted all necessary documents but don't carry a credit card may obtain a bond in the name of the Federal Treasury of Mexico, issued by an authorized company in Mexico. Currently, Mexican bonding companies only operate within the border regions with the exception of *Afianzadora Insurgentes*, which operates in the U.S. through Sanborn Company in McAllen, Texas and other U.S. border states. **To obtain a bond:**

❁Furnish the bonding company with the original and two copies of the driver's resident card or passport, a U.S. Social Security card and a valid driver's license not issued in Mexico.
❁If the vehicle is a company car, a notarized power of attorney must also accompany the necessary paperwork. If the vehicle has not been paid for in full, a letter of authorization must be obtained from the financial institution granting permission to bring the vehicle into Mexico.

HOW MUCH?

Bonds for vehicles that are 1988 and older cost $125. Bonds for newer models will cost approximately 2 to 3 percent of the vehicle's value, plus an insurance fee and taxes. These fees and taxes are not refunded. Bonding companies require a cash deposit in U.S. dollars. Be sure to save the receipt.

The deposit will be refunded through any of Mexico's *Banco del Ejército* banks located at border crossings, 24-hours a day, in U.S. dollars after completion of the return formalities. *Afianzadora Insurgentes* is the only bonding company that has an arrangement with the Banco del Ejército to return deposits. Other bonding companies return deposits only in their own offices during business hours.

DISCOUNT

Some bonding companies offer up to a 50 percent discount on the deposit if the driver also presents the original and two copies of his or her property tax return. The presentation of only an income tax return will entitle the driver to a 30 percent discount.

Bonding companies will reduce the deposit to $100 if the driver owns land in Mexico and can present a photocopy of the property title.

The bond company will require the applicant to sign a note and bond application contract. The bond will be canceled immediately upon the return of the vehicle.

DEPOSIT

Drivers who hold no credit cards and do not wish to obtain a bond from a Mexican bonding company may make a deposit at the Banco del Ejército offices at the border in an amount equal to 100 percent of the vehicle's value. These transactions cost $11.00 and have the same document requirements as other procedures.

The deposit will be refunded only upon completion of the return formalities at the same office at which the deposit was made. Deposits are usually only refunded between 8:30 a.m. and 3 p.m., Monday through Friday.

OBTAINING A DRIVER'S LICENSE

Foreigners may drive anywhere in Mexico, under any tourist or resident status, using their valid driver's license from the U.S. or Canada.

Expatriates must obtain an FM-2 or FM-3 residency status to apply for a Mexican driver's license (see Residency section for more information). Proof of Mexican residency with canceled telephone bills, bank statements etc. is also required, as are four passport-size photographs, two front and two side.

Required Driving Course The Transport Department (Secretaría de Vialidad, Transporte) will only issue a driver's license after the applicant attends a three-hour driving course and passes a written exam, a driving test and an eye examination. The driving course is optional in some states. The entire procedure costs around $20 U.S. and must be completed even if the applicant holds a valid drivers license from his or her home country.

All tests are issued or enacted in Spanish. A translator may help you with the test. If you fail any aspect of the application procedure, you must wait a month to try again. Licenses are issued for four-year periods. All tests must be repeated every time the license is renewed.

THE FINAL WORD

Travelers entering more than 25 kilometers into Mexico must fill out the necessary temporary vehicle import documents. Read carefully the instructions provided by Mexican officials and ensure that the vehicle's title and documents are in order.

Check the expiration date on the temporary import documents. Failure to carefully review all documentation and comply with regulations could lead officials to confiscate the vehicle or slap you with a fine.

The vehicle's owner should be present at all times while the vehicle is in operation on Mexican soil. The owner's absence could result in the vehicle's confiscation.

Vehicles not accompanied by their legal owners will be impounded for illegal importation.

APPENDIX

FOREIGN INVESTMENT LAW OF MEXICO
TITLE FIRST
GENERAL PROVISIONS

CHAPTER I
OBJECT OF THE LAW

ARTICLE 1. Purpose of the Law
This Law is of a public nature and shall be effective throughout [Mexico]. Its purpose is to establish the rules by which foreign investment can be channeled to the country and to ensure that such investments contribute to the national development.

ARTICLE 2. Defined Terms For purposes of this Law, the terms below shall be defined as follows:

I. Commission: National Foreign Investment Commission;

II. Foreign investment:

a) An investment by foreign investors in any percentage of the capital stock of a Mexican corporation;

b) An investment by a Mexican corporation a majority of the capital stock of which is owned by foreign investors; and

c) An investment by foreign investors in the activities and actions contemplated herein.

III. Foreign investor: An individual or legal entity with a nationality other than Mexican; any foreign entity without legal personality;

IV. Registry: National Registry of Foreign Investment;

V. Ministry: Ministry of Trade and Industrial Development;

VI. Restricted Zone: The strip of [Mexican] territory, extending one hundred kilometers from the borders and fifty kilometers from the coasts, which is referred to in section I of Article 27 of the Political Constitution of the United Mexican States; and

VII. Foreign Exclusion Clause: An express covenant or agreement which forms an integral part of the articles of association of a company and establishes that such company shall not accept, directly or indirectly, as partners or shareholders any foreign investors or any companies which permit investment by foreign investors.

ARTICLE 3. Investments by Immigrants For purposes of this Law, investments made by foreigners in the country which have been granted the status of immigrant (*inmigrado*) shall be treated as Mexican investments, except for investments made in the activities contemplated in Titles First and Second herein.

ARTICLE 4. Form of Investments Foreign investors may invest in any percentage of the capital stock of Mexican corporations, acquire fixed assets, open up new areas of economic activity or produce new lines of products, open and operate establishments or expand or relocate existing establishments, except as otherwise provided herein.

The rules concerning investment by foreign investors in the activities of the financial sector as contemplated herein shall apply without prejudice to any rules established by the specific laws for such activities.

CHAPTER II
RESERVED ACTIVITIES

ARTICLE 5. Activities Reserved to the Mexican State The following activities are reserved exclusively to the State as determined by applicable legislation:

I. Petroleum and other hydrocarbons;

II. Basic petrochemicals;

III. Electricity;

IV. Generation of nuclear energy;

V. Radioactive minerals;
VI. Satellite communications;

VII. Telegraphy;

VIII. Radiotelegraphy;

IX. Mail;

X. Railways;

XI. Issuance of bank notes;

XII. Minting of coins;

XIII. Control, supervision and oversight of ports, airports and heliports; and

XIV. Any other areas expressly indicated in the provisions of applicable law.

ARTICLE 6. Activities Reserved to Mexican Nationals The following economic activities and enterprises are reserved exclusively to Mexicans or to Mexican companies having a Foreign Exclusion Clause:

I.   National land transportation of passengers, tourism and cargo, excluding messenger and parcel services;

II.   Retail sale of gasoline and distribution of liquid petroleum gas;

III.   Radio broadcasting and other radio and television services, except those relating to cable television;

IV.   Credit unions;
V.   Development banking institutions, in accordance with applicable law; and

VI.   Professional and technical services expressly referred to in the provisions of applicable law.

Foreign investors may not invest directly in the activities or type of companies mentioned above in this Article, or through trusts, covenants, partnership agreements or articles of association, pyramid schemes, or any other mechanism by which they may acquire control of an investment, except as provided for in Title Fifth herein.

CHAPTER III
ACTIVITIES AND ACQUISITIONS SUBJECT TO SPECIFIC REGULATION

ARTICLE 7. Activities in which Foreign Investment is Subject to Percentage Limits Foreign investment in the economic activities and enterprises mentioned below shall be limited to the following percentages:

I.   Up to 10% in production cooperatives;

II.   Up to 25% in:

a). National air transportation;

b). Transportation by aerotaxis;

c). Specialized air transportation.

III.   Up to 30% in:
a). Companies controlling financial groups;

b). Multiple banking institutions;

c). Securities firms; and

d). Stock exchange specialists.

IV.   Up to 49% in:

a). Insurance companies;

b). Bonding companies;

c). Foreign exchange companies;

d). Bonded warehouses;

e). Financial leasing companies;

f). Financial factoring companies;

g). Limited-purpose financial companies referred to in section IV of Article 103 of the Credit Institutions Law;

h). Companies referred to in Article 12 Bis of the Securities Market Law;

i). Stock which represents the fixed capital of investment companies and operating companies of investment companies;

j). Manufacture and sale of explosives, firearms, cartridges, ammunition and fireworks, excluding the acquisition and utilization of explosives for industrial and extraction activities, or the processing of explosive mixtures for use in connection with such activities;

k). Printing and publication of periodicals for exclusive distribution within the national territory;

l). Series "T" shares of companies holding agricultural, ranching and forestry properties;

m). Cable television;

n). Basic telephone services;

o). Fresh water fishing and coastal fishing in the exclusive economic zone, excluding aquaculture;

p). Port authority administration;

q). Harbor piloting services for ships engaged in cabotage and domestic navigation, in accordance with applicable law;

r). Shipping companies dedicated to commercial for-profit operation of cabotage and domestic navigation services, with the exception of tourist cruise ships and dredging and naval services relating to harbor construction, conservation and port operation;

s). Services relating to railways, including passenger services, maintenance and rehabilitation of rail systems, loading and unloading services, tractor and hauling equipment repair shops, organization and commercial trading of unitary trains, operation of domestic cargo terminals and railroad telecommunications;

t). Supply of fuel and lubricants for ships, airplanes and railroad equipment.

The limitations on foreign investment set forth above cannot be overstepped directly or through trusts, covenants, partnership agreements or articles of association, pyramid schemes or any other mechanism by which control or participation exceeding that which is stated above can be acquired, except as provided in Title Fifth herein.

ARTICLE 8. Activities in which Foreign Investment Above 49% Requires Commission Approval A favorable determination by the Commission is required for any foreign investment in a percentage exceeding 49% in the business activities and types of companies mentioned below:

I.   Harbor services for ships involved in domestic navigation operations such as towing, mooring and lighterage;

II. Shipping companies dedicated exclusively to transoceanic shipping services;

III. Administration of air terminals;

IV. Private educational services at preschool, elementary, junior high school and high school levels (and combinations thereof);

V. Legal services;

VI. Credit information companies;

VII. Securities rating institutions;

VIII. Insurance agents;

IX. Cellular telephone services;

X. Construction and pipelines for the transportation of oil and oil derivatives; and

XI. Drilling of oil and natural gas wells.

ARTICLE 9. Other Foreign Investments Above 49%: When Commission Approval is Required A favorable determination by the Commission is required for any foreign investment, directly or indirectly, in an interest in a Mexican corporation [engaged in an activity other than those mentioned in the preceding Articles] in a percentage exceeding 49% of its capital stock, but only when the total value of the assets of such corpora-

tion, at the time when the application for the acquisition is submitted, exceeds an amount which the Commission shall determine on an annual basis.

TITLE SECOND
ACQUISITION OF REAL PROPERTY AND TRUSTS

CHAPTER I
ACQUISITION OF REAL PROPERTY

ARTICLE 10. Acquisition of Real Property within the Restricted Zone In accordance with the provisions of Section 1 of Article 27 of the Political Constitution of the United Mexican States, Mexican companies which have a Foreign Exclusion Clause or have accepted the agreement referred to in such provisions, can acquire title to real property in the national territory.

In the case of corporations whose articles of association include the agreement referred to in Section 1 of Article 27 of the Constitution, the following shall apply:

I.   They can acquire title to real property located in the Restricted Zone which is designated for non-residential purposes, provided that such acquisitions are recorded with the Ministry of Foreign Affairs;

II.   They can acquire rights to real property in the Restricted Zone which is designated for residential purposes, in accordance with the provisions of the following chapter.

CHAPTER II
TRUSTS AS TO REAL PROPERTY IN THE RESTRICTED ZONE

ARTICLE 11. Trusts Requiring Approval by the Ministry of Foreign Affairs The authorization of the Ministry of Foreign Affairs is required in order for credit institutions to acquire, as trustees, rights with respect to real property located within the Restricted Zone, when the purpose of the trust is to permit the utilization of and profiting from such properties without creating real property rights to them, and the beneficiaries are:

I. Mexican corporations not having a Foreign Exclusion Clause as provided for in section II of Article 10 of this Law; and

II. Foreign individuals or legal entities.

ARTICLE 12. Utilization of and Profiting from Real Property in the Restricted Zone Utilization of and profiting from real property located in the Restricted Zone means the right to use and enjoy the same, including, as the case may be, the benefit of any products and proceeds and, in general, the profits which may result from the lucrative operation and taking advantage thereof through third parties or the fiduciary institution.

ARTICLE 13. Term of the Trust The term of each trust referred to in this chapter shall be a maximum period of fifty years, which period can be extended at the request of the interested party.

The Ministry of Foreign Affairs reserves the right to verify the fulfillment of the conditions pursuant to which the authorizations and registrations referred to in this title are granted.

ARTICLE 14. Permit Approval Process The Ministry of Foreign Affairs shall make determinations with respect to the permits referred to in this Chapter by taking into consideration the economic and social benefits which may inure to the [Mexican] nation as a result of such operations.

Every permit applications which satisfies the indicated requirements must be granted by the Ministry of Foreign Affairs within thirty business days after the date of its submission. The recordations referred to in Section I of Article 10 must be processed within a maximum period of fifteen business days after the submission of the application. Otherwise, the permit or the corresponding registration shall be considered granted.

TITLE THIRD
COMPANIES: ON THEIR INCORPORATION AND AMENDMENT

ARTICLE 15. Incorporation of Companies Requiring Approval by the Ministry of Foreign Affairs The authorization of the Ministry of Foreign Affairs is required for the incorporation of companies. The articles of association of the companies being established must contain the Foreign Exclusion Clause or the agreement provided for in Section I of Article 27 of the Constitution.

ARTICLE 16. Company Amendments Requiring Approval by the Ministry of Foreign Affairs The authorization of the Ministry of Foreign Affairs is required for incorporated companies to change their names, or to modify their Foreign Exclusion Clause so as to allow foreign investment.

TITLE FOURTH
INVESTMENT BY FOREIGN ENTITIES

ARTICLE 17. Qualification of Foreign Companies Without prejudice to the provisions of the international treaties and agreements to which Mexico is a party, in order for foreign entities to perform continuing commercial acts in the Mexican Republic, they must obtain the prior authorization of the Ministry for their registration with the Public Registry of Commerce in accordance with Articles 250 and 251 of the General Law of Mercantile Companies.

Any application for the authorization referred to above which complies with the corresponding requirements must be granted by the Ministry within 15 business days after the date of its submission.

TITLE FIFTH
NEUTRAL INVESTMENT

CHAPTER I
CONCEPT OF
NEUTRAL INVESTMENT

ARTICLE 18. Definition of Neutral Investment Neutral investment is that which is made in Mexican companies or in authorized trusts in accordance with this Title and which shall not be taken into account in determining the percentage of foreign investment in the capital stock of Mexican corporations.

CHAPTER II
NEUTRAL INVESTMENT REPRESENTED BY INSTRUMENTS ISSUED BY FIDUCIARY INSTITUTIONS

ARTICLE 19. Authorization of Fiduciary Institutions The Ministry may authorize fiduciary institutions to issue neutral investment instruments which shall only grant, with regard to companies, financial rights to the holders thereof and, if applicable, limited corporate rights, without granting to the holders any voting rights in the company's Ordinary General Shareholders' Meetings.

CHAPTER III
NEUTRAL INVESTMENT REPRESENTED BY
SPECIAL SERIES OF STOCK

ARTICLE 20. Neutral Investment Securities Investments in stock without voting rights or with limited corporate rights shall be deemed to be neutral investments, provided that the prior approval of the Ministry was obtained and, if applicable, that of the National Securities Commission.

CHAPTER IV
NEUTRAL INVESTMENT IN COMPANIES, CONTROLLING FINANCIAL GROUPS, MULTIPLE BANKING INSTITUTIONS AND SECURITIES FIRMS

ARTICLE 21. Neutral Investment in Companies Controlling Financial Groups, Multiple Banking Institutions and Securities Firms After consultation between the Ministry of Finance and Public Credit and the National Securities Commission, the Ministry may make determinations concerning neutral investments effected through the acquisition of ordinary certificates of participation issued by fiduciary institutions authorized for such purpose, whose capital consists of series "B" shares of the capital stock of companies controlling financial groups or multiple banking institutions or series "A" shares of the capital stock of securities firms.

CHAPTER V
NEUTRAL INVESTMENT MADE BY INTERNATIONAL DEVELOPMENT FINANCE INSTITUTIONS

ARTICLE 22. Neutral Investment by International Development Finance Institutions The Commission may make determina-

tions concerning neutral investments which international development finance institutions seek to make in the capital stock of companies, in accordance with the terms and conditions established to this effect by the regulation promulgated under this Law.

TITLE SIXTH
NATIONAL FOREIGN INVESTMENT COMMISSION

CHAPTER I
STRUCTURE OF THE COMMISSION

ARTICLE 23. Composition of the Commission The Commission shall be composed of the Ministers of the Interior; Foreign Affairs; Finance and Public Credit; Social Development; Energy, Mines and Parastatal Industries; Trade and Industrial Development; Communications and Transportation; and Tourism, each of whom can designate a deputy Minister as his or her representative. Also, any authorities with competence in the matters involved can be invited to participate in the sessions of the Commission.

ARTICLE 24. SECOFI and the Commission The Commission shall be chaired by the Minister of Trade and Industrial Development and shall have an Executive Secretary and a Committee of Representatives to carry out its daily functions.

ARTICLE 25. Composition of the Committee of Representatives The committee of representatives shall be composed of the public officials designated by each of the Ministers who belong to the Commissions and shall have the powers delegated to it by the Commission.

CHAPTER II
AUTHORITY OF
THE COMMISSION

ARTICLE 26. Authority of the Commission The Commission shall have the following authority:

I. To establish the policy guidelines relating to foreign investment and to design the mechanisms for promoting investment in Mexico;

II. To determine, through the Ministry, the merits and, as applicable, the terms and conditions of foreign investment in the activities or in the situations subject to specific regulation under Articles 8 and 9 of this Law;

III. To provide mandatory consultation in the area of foreign investment for the various departments and agencies of the Federal Republic Administration;

IV. To establish the criteria for the application of the legal and regulatory provisions in the area of foreign investment through the issuance of general resolutions; and

V. Any other authority which would inure to it in accordance with this law.

ARTICLE 27. Authority of the Executive Secretary The Executive Secretary of the Commission shall have the following authority:

I. To represent the Commission;

II. To give notice of the resolutions of the Commission through the Ministry;

III. To carry out the studies entrusted to it by the Commission;

IV. To submit to the Mexican Congress an annual statistical report regarding foreign investment activities in the country, including the economic sectors and the regions in which such investments are made; and

V. Any other authority which would inure to it in accordance with this Law.

CHAPTER III
OPERATION OF
THE COMMISSION

ARTICLE 28. Decisions of the Commission The Commission must rule on the applications submitted for its consideration not more than 45 business days after the date such application was submitted, pursuant to the terms established by the Regulation of this Law.

In the event the Commission does not make a decision with respect to any application within the allocated period, the application shall be deemed to be approved in accordance with the terms thereof. At the express request of an interested party, the Ministry shall issue the corresponding authorization.

ARTICLE 29. Factors to be Considered by the Commission In order to evaluate the applications submitted for its consideration, the Commission shall consider the following criteria:

I. The impact on employment and the training of workers;
II. The technological contribution;

III. Compliance with rules relating to environmental matters as contained in the applicable ecological laws; and

IV. In general, the contribution to development of the competitiveness of the productive base of the country.

The Commission, when deciding upon the merits of an application, may only impose requirements that do not distort international trade.

ARTICLE 30. National Security The Commission may prevent acquisitions by foreign investors for reasons of national security.

TITLE SEVENTH
NATIONAL REGISTRY OF
FOREIGN INVESTMENT

ARTICLE 31. Structure of the Registry The Registry shall not be of a public nature, and shall be divided into sections established by its internal rules which shall determine its organization as well as the information that should be filed with the Registry.

ARTICLE 32. Registrations with the Registry The following must register themselves with the Registry:

I. Mexican companies with foreign investors;
II. Foreign individuals and entities carrying out commercial activities in the Mexican Republic, and branch offices of foreign investors established in the country; and

III. Stock or partnership trusts, real property and neutral investment trusts in which beneficial rights are held by foreign investors.

The obligation to register shall be the responsibility of the individuals or legal entities referred to in sections I and II above and, with respect to section III, the obligation to register shall apply to the fiduciary institutions. The registration must be made within 40 business days after the date on which the company was organized or the foreign investment was permitted; on which the formalization or legalization of the documents relating to the foreign company was completed; or on which the respective trust was created or the beneficial ownership interests were transferred to the foreign investor.

ARTICLE 33. Registration Receipts The Registry shall issue registration receipts when the following data is contained in the application:

I. With respect to sections I and II [above]:

a). Name, firm name or trade name, address, date of organization if relevant, and principal business activity to be performed;

b). Name and address of the legal representative;

c). Name and address of persons authorized to hear and receive notifications;

d). Name, firm name or trade name, nationality and immigration status if relevant, address of each foreign investor in or outside the country and the percentage of the corresponding investment;

e). Amount of capital subscribed and paid or subscribed and payable;

f). Estimated date of the beginning of operations and approximate amount of the total investment (broken down into a schedule).

II. With respect to section III [above]:

a). Name of the fiduciary institution;

b). Name, firm name or trade name, address and nationality of each foreign investor or foreign investor beneficiary;

c). Name, firm name or trade name, address and nationality of each foreign investor or designated trustee of a foreign investor;

d). Date of creation, purpose and term of the trust; and

e). Description, value, function and, if relevant, location of the assets held in trust.

Once any registration receipts and renewals have been issued, the Registry reserves the right to solicit clarifications with respect to the information submitted.

Any modification of the information submitted in accordance with this Article must be communicated to the Registry in accordance with its internal rules.

ARTICLE 34. Instruction to Notaries Public With respect to any organization, modification, transformation, merger, split, dissolution and liquidation of mercantile businesses, civil associations or corporations and, in general, in all legal actions and proceedings where they may appear in person or by representation, notaries public shall demand that such persons (or their representatives) as are obligated to register with the Registry pursuant to the terms of Article 32 of this Law, submit evidence of their registration with the Registry, and in the event that the registration is still being processed, that they submit evidence of the filing of the corresponding application. If no such evidence is submitted, notaries public may legalize the respective public instrument but shall inform the Registry of such omission within ten business days after the date on which the instrument was legalized.

ARTICLE 35. Registration Renewals The persons required to register with the Registry must renew their registrations annually, and for such purpose it shall suffice to submit a financial and economic questionnaire in accordance with the internal rules of the Commission.

ARTICLE 36. Government Reporting Requirements The federal, state and municipal authorities are required to provide the Ministry with the necessary report and certifications to enable it to comply with its functions in accordance with this Law and the regulatory provisions thereof.

TITLE EIGHTH
SANCTIONS

ARTICLE 37. Revocation of Authorizations In the event of actions contrary to the provisions of this Law, the Ministry may revoke the authorizations granted.

The acts, agreements, partnership agreements or articles of association which are declared to be void by the Ministry, as contrary to the provisions of this Law, shall have no legal effect between the parties and shall be unenforceable with respect to third parties.

ARTICLE 38. Other Sanctions Violations of the provisions of this Law and the regulatory provisions

promulgated hereunder shall be punished as follows:

I. In the event that the foreign investor carries out activities, acquisitions or any other act for which a favorable resolution of the Commission is required, without such authorization having been previously obtained, a fine of 1,000 to 5,000 salaries shall be imposed;

II. In the event that foreign legal entities perform on a regular basis commercial activities in the Mexican Republic without having obtained the prior authorization of the Ministry, a fine of 500 to 1,000 salaries shall be imposed;

III. In the event of actions in violation of the provisions of this Law and the regulatory provisions promulgated hereunder with respect to neutral investment, a fine of 100 to 300 salaries shall be imposed;

IV. In the event of an omission, late filing, submission of incomplete or incorrect information with respect to registration requirements, reporting or notification to the Registry, a fine of 30 to 100 salaries shall be imposed;

V. In the event of sham activities with the purpose of allowing the enjoyment or the sale of real property in the Restricted Zone to foreign individuals or legal entities or Mexican corporations that do not have a Foreign Exclusion Clause, in violation of the provisions of Titles Second and Third of this Law, the violator shall be assessed a fine up to the total amount of the transaction; and

VI. Other violations of this Law and the regulatory provisions promulgated hereunder shall be punished with a fine ranging from 100 to 1,000 salaries.

For purposes of this Article, salary shall mean the minimum general daily wage in force in the Federal District at the time of the violation.

In determining and imposing sanctions, the affected party must be first heard and, in the event of monetary sanctions, the nature of the violation must be taken into consideration, as well as the seriousness of the actions, the economic ability of the offender to pay, the lapse of time that ran between the date of requirement should have been complied with and the time of its compliance or regularization, and the total value of the transaction.

The Ministry shall be responsible for imposing the sanctions, except for the violation referred to in section V of this Article and other violations relating to Titles Second and Third of this Law, the sanctions for which shall be imposed by the Ministry of Foreign Affairs.

The imposition of sanctions referred to in this Title shall be without prejudice to any other civil or criminal liability, as the case may be.

ARTICLE 39. Instruction to Notaries Public Notaries public shall report, insert or add to the official file or appendix of the instruments which they prepare, the functions included in the authorizations that must be issued pursuant to the terms of this Law. When they legalize instruments in which they do not report such authorizations, they will subject themselves to such sanctions as may be specified in the laws governing notaries public and the Federal Law of Notaries Public.

TRANSITIONAL PROVISIONS

ONE. This Law shall take effect on the day following its publication in the Diario Oficial de la Federación.

TWO. The following are hereby repealed:

I. The Law for the Promotion of Mexican Investment and Regulation of Foreign Investment, published in the Diario Oficial de la Federación on March 9, 1973;

II. The Organic Law of Section I of Article 27 of the Constitution, published in the Diario Oficial de la Federación on January 21, 1926;

III. The Decree establishing the temporary necessity of obtaining a permit in order for foreigners to acquire assets, and in order to establish and modify Mexican companies that have or could have foreign partners, which was published in the

230 APPENDIX: FOREIGN INVESTMENT LAW OF MEXICO

Diario Oficial de la Federación on July 7, 1944.

THREE. The following are hereby amended:

I. Articles 46 and 47 of the Federal Law on Firearms and Explosives published in the Diario Oficial de la Federación on January 11, 1972;

II. All legal, regulatory, and administrative provisions general in nature that are inconsistent with this Law.

FOUR. During the time the regulations under this Law are being prepared, the regulation under the Law to Promote Mexican Investment and Regulate Foreign Investment published in the Diario Oficial de la Federación on May 15, 1989 shall remain in force to the extent non inconsistent with this Law.

FIVE. Foreign investors and companies with foreign investors which; at the time of publication of this Law, have already established schedules, complied with requirements and made commitments before the Commission, its Executive Secretary or the Executive Office for Foreign Investment of the Ministry, may submit for consideration by such Executive Office an application for exemption from compliance, to which such administrative unit must respond within 45 business days after the date of submission of such application. Foreign investors who do not take

advantage of the possibility of such exemption must comply with the commitments previous set by the Commission and the aforementioned persons and public entities.

SIX. Activities such as international land transportation of passengers, tourism and cargo between points in the Mexican territory, as well as administrative services relating to passenger trucking centers and auxiliary services are reserved exclusively to Mexicans and to Mexican companies having a Foreign Exclusion Clause.
Notwithstanding the foregoing, foreign investors may acquire interests in the above mentioned business activities in accordance with the following provisions:

I. As of December 18, 1995, up to 49% of the capital of Mexican companies;

II. As of January 1, 2001, up to 51% of the capital of Mexican companies without the necessity of obtaining the prior approval of the Commission.

III. As of January 1, 2004, up to 100% of the capital of Mexican companies without the necessity of obtaining the prior approval of the Commission.

SEVEN. Foreign investors may acquire interests in up to 49% of the capital of Mexican companies devoted to the manufacture and assembly of parts, equipment and accessories for the automotive industry, without prejudice to the provisions of the Decree for the Development and Modernization of the Automotive Industry. As of January 1, 1999, foreign investors may acquire up to 100% of the capital of Mexican companies without the necessity of obtaining the prior approval of the Commission.

EIGHT. With respect to services relating to videotext and telephone switching systems, foreign investors may acquire interests of up to 49% of the capital of Mexican companies. From and after July 1, 1995, foreign investors may acquire interests of up to 100% in the capital of companies dedicated to such services, without the necessity of obtaining the prior approval of the Commission.

NINE. The prior approval of the Commission is required in order for foreign investors to invest in more than 49% of the capital of companies engaged in any of the following activities:

I.   Building, construction and installation of construction sites;

II.   Construction of pipelines for the transportation of petroleum and byproducts; and

III.   Drilling of oil and gas wells.

With respect to the business activities mentioned in section I, from and after January 1, 1999

foreign investors may invest in up to 100% in the capital of Mexican companies dedicated to such activities without the necessity of obtaining the prior approval of the Commission.

TEN. For purposes of the provisions of Article 9, and while the Commission is determining the amount of the total value of the assets referred to in the above-referenced Article, such amount shall be deemed to be 85,000,000 New Pesos.

ELEVEN. Foreign investors and Mexican companies with a foreign admittance clause who, on the effective date of this law, are the beneficiaries of real properties held in trust in the Restricted Zone shall be subject to the provisions of Chapter II of Title Second, to the extent that they benefit therefrom.

[January 7, 1994]

DISCLAIMER: This translation from Spanish to English has been prepared for the convenience of clients and friends of Carlsmith Ball, which has endeavored to create a readable and accurate translation. However, there are particular difficulties inherent in translating legislation, where in some respects the legislative intent may not be clear in the original text. Carlsmith Ball disclaims any liability for any failure by the firm to convey in this translation the precise equivalent in English of any portion of the legislation, or of the legislative intent behind any provision thereof. This translation is not intended to express any legal opinion or opinions on any aspect of the legislation. Neither Carlsmith Ball García Cacho y Asociados, S.C., nor Carlsmith Ball Wichman Murray Case & Ichiki nor any partner or employee of either thereof is licensed as a translator or interpreter by any licensing authority.

NAFTA BENEFITS FOR SMALL BUSINESSES

The North American Free Trade Agreement (NAFTA) provides signifi-cant new commercial opportunities in Mexico and Canada for U.S. small businesses by eliminating barriers to trade between the United States and its first and third largest trading partners.

There are approximately 10,000 firms in the United States that export to Mexico. Most of these companies are small- and medium-sized busi-nesses. While major multinational firms account for the largest share of U.S. exports to Canada and Mexico in terms of value, NAFTA enables small- and medium-sized businesses to expand their share.

President Clinton will submit legislation to Congress to implement the NAFTA this fall, now that the supplemental agreements on environment, la-bor and import surges are complete. The supplemental agreements are:

•Establish a Commission on Environmental Cooperation to ensure envi-ronmental cooperation and strengthen enforcement of domestic envi-ronmental laws, through the use of trade sanctions and other penalties.

•Establish a Commission on Labor Cooperation to promote the improvement of working conditions and living standards and strengthen the enforcement of domestic labor laws through trade sanctions and other penalties.

•Establish a working group to consult regarding the use of NAFTA safe-guard procedures.

Together, the NAFTA and the supplemental agreements promote fair and open competition based on innovation and rising levels of productivity and quality — principles on which our mutual prosperity depends.

BENEFITS TO U.S. SMALL BUSINESS

NAFTA eliminates numerous tariff and non-tariff barriers in Mexico and Canada to U.S. exports of goods and services, providing increased market op-portunities for U.S. small business. Further, the elimination or simplification of numerous procedures, from customs regulations to standards, enables small businesses to take advantage of the Mexican market. Finally, NAFTA's invest-ment provisions provide fair treatment for NAFTA investors interested in in-vesting in Mexico, and removes barriers, such as requirements for joint venture partners or export performance requirements, that discourage small investors.

TARIFFS

Tariffs in Mexico currently range up to 25 percent. NAFTA immediately eliminates tariffs on 50 percent of U.S. product categories going to Mexico; within five years, 65 percent of U.S. industrial product categories will enter Mexico duty free. Within 10 years, all U.S. industrial products will enter Mexico duty free. For those U.S. industries which are highly sensitive to imports, including such products as certain watches, household glassware, ceramic tiles, and footwear, duties will be eliminated in 15 years.

Tariffs have often kept small businesses out of export markets because they do not have the market clout, cost advantages or resources to overcome these barriers. The elimination of tariffs in Mexico could give U.S. exporters as much as a 25 percent cost advantage over their non-NAFTA competitors. The tariff elimination schedule negotiated under the U.S.-Canada Free Trade Agreement (CFTA) will continue; duties between the United States and Canada will be fully eliminated by 1998.

SERVICES

Under NAFTA, service providers no longer have to establish in Mexico to provide services. This is of particular benefit to small businesses, which often cannot justify the capital expense of establishing abroad. Under NAFTA, a small firm will be able to expand its customer base into Mexico and Canada without having to hire additional personnel or open a branch office there.

The elimination of barriers to cross-border provision of services allows service providers to choose the method of delivery that is most economical for them. Service areas particularly benefiting from these provisions are accounting, architecture, transportation, telecommunications, environmental consulting, and software development.

SAFEGUARDS AGAINST IMPORT SURGES

For certain industries, NAFTA provides for the gradual, as opposed to all-at-once, elimination of tariffs so that industries have sufficient time to adjust to increased import competition. Under the safeguard mechanism, U.S. tariffs can be "snapped-back" to their Most-Favored-Nation levels for up to three years if increased imports seriously injure or threaten U.S. manufacturers. This option is available against any particular good only once during the transition period. General U.S. import relief provisions concerning imports from the world remain available to U.S. industries.

President Clinton has also stated that he intends to have a sufficiently funded worker retraining program available for workers who may lose their jobs for any reason, including imports.

STANDARDS

Small businesses often have difficulty determining what standards and labeling requirements apply to their products. Lack of transparency in the development and issuance of standards or labeling requirements can frustrate small businesses that do not possess the resources to conduct a bureaucratic search in a foreign language.

NAFTA's Standards Chapter contains three key principles. The first is that goods or specified services from the other two countries are, with respect to standards-related measures, treated no less favorably than similar goods or services of national origin, and similar goods or services from non-NAFTA countries. Second, standards cannot be used as a disguised barrier for trade, for example, by being designed so that foreign products cannot meet them. Finally, the procedures to develop standards will be transparent, and all relevant information will be made available to interested parties.

When the development of new standards is underway, interested parties in all three countries will receive notice at the same time that the process has begun. This will allow for input from U.S. firms at a far earlier stage in the development of a new standard than under the GATT process. U.S. firms have the right to participate in the standards-development process, either as individuals or through an industry association, when another NAFTA party allows its firms to participate.

Finally, NAFTA requires a full 60-day comment period on all draft standards. Mexico has actually exceeded its NAFTA obligations and now provides a 90-day comment period on all draft standards.

The NAFTA Standards Chapter also requires all three governments to maintain an inquiry point to respond to requests about standards from the other governments and private companies. Countries are also required to make standards-related documents containing standards publicly available for a nominal charge. This is especially good news for small businesses that will now have guaranteed access to accurate and up-to-date information on Mexico's laws with a minimum of effort.

GOVERNMENT PROCUREMENT

The government sector is one of Mexico's major markets. NAFTA's provisions on government procurement open this market and provide certainty to potential government suppliers.

NAFTA establishes thresholds above which suppliers of North American goods and services must be allowed to participate in the bidding process on a no less favorable basis than suppliers of domestic goods and services. For procurements by Mexican government agencies, the thresholds for goods and services is $50,000 and the threshold for construction services is $6.5 million. Canadian government agencies will have a $25,000 threshold for goods, a $50,000 threshold for services, and $6.5 million for construction.

For state-owned enterprises of Mexico and Canada, the threshold is $250,000 for goods and services, and $8 million for construction services.

NAFTA's coverage of trade in services, including construction, computer software design and environmental consulting, is expected to result in substantially increased opportunities for U.S. exports. NAFTA provides for transparent government tendering procedures and a predictable procurement system of competitive bidding opportunities. A bid-challenge mechanism will enable suppliers to request an independent review of the bidding process and the awarding of contracts.

NAFTA allows the United States to continue its programs that set aside certain government procurements for small and minority businesses. To enable small business to take advantage of NAFTA's government procurement provisions, the governments will agree to jointly promote procurement opportunities for small business.

RULES OF ORIGIN

NAFTA rules of origin ensure that tariff benefits accrue only to U.S., Canadian and Mexican goods, rather than goods produced outside the region. Only North American products, as defined by the rules of origin, are eligible for preferential tariff treatment under the agreement. NAFTA rules of origin are decidedly easier for companies to use than the U.S.-Canada Free Trade Agreement rules of origin. There are now fewer rules requiring cost accounting, and those that do require such calculations are based on much simpler formulas.

Products qualify for NAFTA tariff status if they are wholly North American. Products containing non-North American material may qualify for NAFTA tariff status by undergoing significant processing in North America. Significant processing is measured by "tariff-shifts" in the Harmonized System (HS) tariff classification, generally at the chapter (HS 2 digit classification) or heading level (4 digit), and less frequently, at the subheading level (6 digits). This essentially means that non-North American inputs must be classified outside of specified tariff numbers in order for the product to qualify for NAFTA preference.

A "regional value content" test is a supplemental criterion in some cases. If the "transaction value" method is used, the regional content requirement is 60 percent. The regional content requirement is 50 percent if the net cost method is used. The transaction value method is based on the price paid or payable for a good. This approach avoids the need for complex cost accounting systems. The net cost method is based on total cost less the costs of royalties, sales promotion, and packing and shipping and limits interest costs. Producers generally have the option to use either method. However, only the net cost method may be used where the transaction value is not acceptable under the Customs Valuation Code.

A *de minims* provision, created in response to industry advice, gives producers more flexibility. The *de minimis* rule prevents small amounts (up to 7 percent of the value of the good) of non-originating material from disqualifying the exported good.

CUSTOMS ADMINISTRATION

Under NAFTA, Mexico, Canada and the United States agree to implement many uniform customs procedures and regulations. The reformed customs provisions benefit U.S. companies by ensuring predictability and transparency in the exporting process. Small- to medium-sized companies will especially benefit, since they often have limited resources to devote to dealing with the myriad customs issues. Uniform procedures ensure that exporters who market their product in more than one NAFTA country will not have to adapt to multiple customs regimes.

Many procedures governing rules-of-origin documentation, record-keeping and origin-verification are the same for all three NAFTA countries. The customs administrations in all three countries will use the same NAFTA certificate-of-origin form. In addition, Mexican, Canadian, and U.S. customs administrations will issue advance rulings, upon request, on whether or not a product qualifies for tariff preference under the NAFTA rules of origin. This requirement removes a great deal of uncertainty from the exporting process. To further assist the business community, each NAFTA country has made special provisions to respond to rules of origin inquiries through a NAFTA Customs Help Desk. (See table for telephone numbers.)

INTELLECTUAL PROPERTY RIGHTS

NAFTA provides better intellectual property protection than any other international agreement signed by the United States. According to the agreement, products are patentable for a 20-year term from the date of filing in Canada or Mexico, or a 17-year term from the date of grant in the United States. Very few inventions are completely excluded from patentability. Compulsory licenses for patents can be issued only in limited circumstances. Small firms with good ideas have been vulnerable in the past to Mexico's broadly interpreted compulsory licensing regime because they were unable to invest in Mexico and meet the patent working requirements. NAFTA now allows firms to meet the working requirement with imported products, and severely limits Mexico's ability to issue compulsory licenses.

Trademarks are issued for 10-year, renewable terms. Service marks and certification marks, indicating membership or participation in a certification scheme that guarantees a specified level of services, are eligible for registration. Collective marks, representing groups of businesses, are also eligible.

Copyright protection extends to computer software, compilations and data bases and is available to all copyrighted works upon creation of the work; no registrations in Mexico are required for copyright protection.

NAFTA is the first international agreement to afford significant protection for trade secrets. This is good news for small companies that often depend on the rapid development and exploitation of new technologies and techniques. The patent process is often too slow to afford much protection for such firms, and trade-secret protection is critical.

NAFTA also contains extensive provisions on IPR enforcement, including civil and administrative procedures, provisional remedies, criminal penalties and border enforcement. These IPR enforcement provisions should help to ensure that NAFTA yields real benefits for U.S. firms.

FOREIGN INVESTMENT

NAFTA phases out most trade-distorting performance requirements and immediately eliminates trade balancing as a condition for automatic government approval of foreign investment. NAFTA also eliminates other performance requirements such as domestic sales restrictions, local content rules, technology transfer, product mandating, and export performance.

Mexico must eliminate all performance requirements on maquiladora operations within seven years. Mexico must gradually increase the amount of maquiladora production that can be sold in the domestic market until such sales restrictions are removed in seven years. During this seven-year period, restrictions on sales by maquiladoras into the Mexican market will be lifted by 5 percent annually from a base of 55 percent in the first year of NAFTA implementation until full access is gained in year seven. The NAFTA's strict limitation on duty drawback removes other adverse trade distortions associated with the maquiladoras.

NAFTA enables investors, without government approval, to own 100 percent of the ownership interest in virtually all new enterprises considered to be in the small business sector. NAFTA investment rules substantially improve the current situation in which foreign investors are limited to a 49 percent equity share in these operations unless they meet certain government mandated performance requirements and restrictions.

Each NAFTA party has agreed to accord non-discriminatory treatment to NAFTA-region investors, with limited exceptions. Canada maintains the right to approve direct acquisitions of existing companies exceeding C$150 million. Mexico also maintains the right to approve acquisitions exceeding $25 million, rising to $150 million nine years after the implementation of NAFTA. The $150 million and C$150 million approval levels will be adjusted annually for inflation and economic growth.

NAFTA accords investors, at minimum, treatment in accordance with international law.

Investors have the right to appoint senior managers of their choice, regardless of nationality.

Investors have the right to transfer profits, dividends, interest, capital, royalty payments, and other remittances relating to the investment without delay, in a freely usable currency, and at the market rate of exchange.

Expropriation can occur only for a public purpose and on a non-discriminatory basis. Investors have the right to prompt, adequate and effective compensation in the event of an expropriation. The compensation must be freely transferable.

NAFTA grants investors, at their option, access to international arbitration of disputes with host governments concerning breaches of NAFTA's investment obligations. The arbitration provision is an important development in U.S. trade relations with Latin America, as certain countries in that region have denied foreign investors such access.

ANTIDUMPING AND COUNTERVAILING DUTIES

Under NAFTA, Mexico has agreed to make far-reaching changes to its antidumping (AD) and countervailing duty (CVD) laws and practices to provide full due-process guarantees and effective judicial review to U.S. exporters. This means that U.S. exporters to Mexico will gain the same rights in Mexican AD/CVD proceedings that Mexican exporters have under the U.S. system and will help ensure that Mexican AD/CVD cases against U.S. products are carried out in an impartial and transparent manner.

NAFTA results in no substantive changes to U.S. AD and CVD law. Disputes involving AD or CVD laws generally will be addressed by binational panels. The panel's mandate is limited to whether decisions rendered by Mexico, the U.S. or Canada are consistent with their domestic law.

TRANSPORTATION AND DISTRIBUTION

By eliminating the need to "hands off" cargo to Mexican carriers at the border, NAFTA's land transport provisions will provide major benefits to U.S. exporters. As the schedule of liberalization is implemented, U.S. truck companies will, for the first time, have the right to use their own drivers and equipment for cross-border cargo and passenger service to Mexico. This will enable a U.S. trucking company to pick up cargo anywhere in the United States, deliver it anywhere in Mexico and back haul cargo from Mexico to the United States.

Eliminating the need to stop at the border to transfer goods to Mexican carriers and allowing back hauling of cargo reduce shipping times and costs and increase reliability of service. These benefits will enhance the competitiveness of U.S. goods in the Mexican market. This provision is of special interest to small businesses located near the border that can use their own U.S.-licensed trucks and drivers to service customers on the Mexican side of the border.

NAFTA maintains high U.S. safety standards. Mexican carriers operating in the United States must meet the same safety standards as U.S. carriers. All foreign drivers must meet the same qualification and licensing standards as U.S. drivers, and use vehicles that meet U.S. size and weight limits. NAFTA establishes a Land Transportation Standards Subcommittee to make safety and technical standards throughout North America compatible.

NAFTA's investment provisions allow small- and medium-sized businesses to establish warehouses and distribution centers without prior government approval. This is of particular benefit to companies that need to warehouse products or spare parts in Mexico and Canada to better service those markets. Even for small firms without the resources to invest in warehouses, this provision will ensure increased warehouse capacity available for lease.

PRIVATE COMMERCIAL DISPUTES

NAFTA requires that each party to the Agreement have in place procedures to enforce arbitration clauses in commercial contracts, and for the recognition and enforcement of arbitral awards. This provision will make arbitration a viable alternative to the use of local courts.

NAFTA also requires each country to promote and facilitate the use of alternative dispute settlement mechanisms, such as arbitration, mediation and "mini-trials," to settle international commercial disputes between private firms. Alternative dispute settlement procedures have often proved to be more effective and less costly than litigating through the courts.

ASSISTANCE FOR SMALL BUSINESS

The Department of Commerce has several programs to help small- to medium-sized businesses export to Mexico. The Department can assist in finding agents and distributors for U.S. products, provide marketing information and provide financial background checks on potential customers. The Department also provides industry sector assistance, which includes counseling, industry-specific trade promotion events, and information on prospects for U.S. industries and trade opportunities.

Small businesses can incorporate this wealth of knowledge into their own company marketing decision-making. For information, call the Trade Information Center at 1-800-872-8723.

The U.S. Department of Commerce operates a trade center in Mexico City which exhibits U.S. products. Of the approximately 450 firms that participated in U.S. Trade Center events, at least 80 percent were small- and medium-sized companies. Rep-Com, a show which takes place semi-annually, is specifically designed for small- to medium-sized companies new to export trade.

A new program at the American Embassy in Mexico City identifies key contacts and commercial and project opportunities in 19 "second-tier cities" (not Mexico City, Monterrey or Guadalajara). These cities may offer better opportunities for small firms to penetrate markets and find niches.

The Department of Commerce's automated information system, Flash Facts, will send information on a wide range of topics on Mexico and Canada seven days a week, 24 hours a day, to any facsimile machine in the United States. The phone numbers are 202-482-4464 (Office of Mexico) and 202-482-3101 (Office of Canada). To order the menu, dial 0101 (Mexico) and 0100 (Canada) from a touch-tone phone, and enter the fax number to which the documents will be sent.

The U.S. Department of Commerce's Office of Canada provides U.S. companies with a variety of services to assist them beginning or increasing export sales to Canada. These services include customized business counseling, publications on export procedures and marketing opportunities in Canada, topical bulletins on commonly asked business questions, and a unique Canada First! Seminar series which introduces U.S. business men and women to exporting to Canada by providing hands-on training, usually at a U.S./Canadian border location.

The Department of Commerce offers additional assistance for small businesses through its Small Business Program, which focuses on trade issues concerning small business and ensures that small business issues are factored into trade policy decisions. For more information, call (202) 482-4792.

More information on U.S. Department of Commerce services can be obtained from a Department of Commerce District Office.

SMALL BUSINESS

For more information about how NAFTA can benefit small business contact one of the following sources:

•U.S. Department of Commerce	
Office of Mexico	(202) 482-0300
•"Flash Facts" Information Line	(202) 482-4464
Office of Canada	(202) 482-3103
•"Flash Facts" Information Line	(202) 482-3101
•Trade Advisory Center	
Sylvia Prosak	(202) 482-4792
Industrial Trade Staff	(202) 482-3703
United States Customs Service	
NAFTA Help Desk	(202) 692-0066
"Flash Facts" Information Line	(202) 692-1692
Mexican Government NAFTA	
Hotline	(011-525) 211-3545
Faxline	(011-525) 256-4737

SUGGESTED READING

Offshore Money Book by Arnold L Cornez, J.D., International Publishing Chicago

El Ojo del Lago (Lake Chapala Weekly) P.O. Box #279, Chapala, Jalisco, Mexico 45900

The Offshore Entrepreneur, by Adam Starchild, First Street Press

The Complete Guide to Offshore Money Havens, by Jerome Schneider, Prima Publishing

Escape From America, by Roger Gallo, Manhattan Loft Publishing

Atencion San Miguel is a weekly English Language newspaper. To order, write Biblioteca Publica, Apartado Postal 119, San Miguel de Allende, Gto. Mexico

Mexico Finance and *Mexico Business* are two good magazines covering the Mexican investment sector. 3033 Chimney Rock #300, Houston, TX 77056-6239

Business Mexico is a magazine published by the American Chamber of Commerce of Mexico contains good general business information. Lucerna 78, Col. Juarez, 06600, Mexico D.F.

Mexico City Times, a daily English language newspaper. U.S. office: 2300 South Broadway, Los Angeles, CA 90007, Tel: (213) 747-7547, Fax (213) 747-2489

Mexletter, monthly investment letter. Mexus Group, Apartado Postal 10711, Mexico D.F. 11000. Tel: (525) 533-3600

The Complete Guide to Doing Business in Mexico is another good business book that is a must-read for the serious investor. AMACON 135 West 50th Street, New York, NY 10020.

Doing Business in Mexico is a good book for business people. Prima Publishing, P.O. Box 1260 BK, Rockling, CA 95677.

How to Buy Real Estate in Mexico is a must-read for the serious real estate investor. Law Mexico Publishing, 539 Telegraph Canyon Road #787, Chula Vista, CA 91910-6497.

Transitions Abroad, a bimonthly magazine on learning, living and working overseas, P.O. Box 1300, Amhurst, MA 01004.

SOURCES USED
IN COMPILING THIS BOOK

Global Paradox, by John Nasibitt. Avon Book

Latin Trade magazine, Various issues October through December 1997

Mexico Business, World Trade Press

Transitions Abroad, Magazine, various issues 1997

MRTA Mexico Living and *Travel Newsletter,* Various issues 1997

Work Your Way Around the World, Susan Griffith

Money Magazine. Various issues 1997

Traveler's Medical Alert to Mexico, ICS Books Inc.

Traveler's Guide to Mexico

MEXICAN EMBASSIES & CONSULATES IN THE U.S.

Embassy of Mexico, U.S.
Washington, DC 20006
Tel: (202) 728-1633/36/45/94

Alburquerque
Mexican Consulate in
Alburquerque, NM 78102
Tel: (505) 247-2139/47, 242-7566

Atlanta
Mexico Consulate
Atlanta, GA 30305
Tel: (404) 266-0777/1204/1614/1908/13

Boston
Mexican Consulate
Boston, MA 02116
Tel: (617) 426-4942/8782, 482-4181

Chicago
Mexican Consulate
Chicago, IL. 60601
Tel: (312) 855-0056/1380/84

Dallas
Mexican Consulate
Dallas, TX 75247
Tel: (214) 630-1604/7341/43, 631-7772

Denver
Mexican Consulate
Denver, CO. 80206
Tel: (303) 331-1110/12/1867/69/71

Detroit
Mexican Consulate
Detroit, MI. 48243-1801
Tel: (313) 567-7709/13/26

Houston
Mexican Consulate
Houston, TX 77098
Tel: (713) 524-2300/1301/3988/2459

Laredo
Mexican Consulate
Laredo, TX 78040
Tel: (210) 723-0990/6360/69

Miami
Mexican Consulate
Miami, FL 33126
Tel: (305) 716-4977 to 79

New Orleans
Mexican Consulate
New Orleans, LA 70130
Tel: (504) 522-3596/97/3601/08

New York
Mexican Consulate
New York, NY 10017
Tel: (212) 689-0456 to 60,
725-8476

Philadelphia
Mexican Consulate
Philadelphia, PA 19106
Tel: (215) 625-4897, 922-4312

Phoenix
Mexican Consulate
Phoenix, AZ 85015
Tel: (602) 242-2294/2363/7398

Portland
Mexican Consulate
Portland, OR 97205
Tel: (503) 274-7442/50/9973

Sacramento
Mexican Consulate
Sacramento, CA 95827
Tel: (916) 363-3885/0403/7791

St. Louis
Mexican Consulate
Saint Louis, MO 63101
Tel: (314) 463-3075/3233/3426

Salt Lake City
Mexican Consulate
Salt Lake City, UT 84111
Tel: (801) 521-8502 to 03

San Antonio
Mexican Consulate
San Antonio, TX 78205
Tel: (210) 227-9145/46/59,
227-1085

San Diego
Mexican Consulate
San Diego, CA 92101
Tel: (619) 231-8414/9741/5843

San Francisco
Mexican Consulate
San Francisco, CA 9410
Tel: (415) 392-3604/5554/6576

San Juan
Mexican Consulate
San Juan, PR 00918
Tel: (809) 764-0258/8923/8935

Seattle
Mexican Consulate
Seattle, WA 92121
Tel: (206) 448-3526/6819/8435 ext. 10

Tucson
Mexican Consulate
Tucson, AZ 85701
Tel: (520) 882-5595/96/8852

U.S. TRADE OFFICES IN MEXICO

The trade offices provide information and assistance to those who need to contact Mexican companies, organize trade missions, and promote their product in Mexico and vice-versa.

Arizona
Mexico, D.F
Tel: (525) 566-9850
E-mail:
dbarreir@infocel.net.mex

Arkansas
Mexico, D.F.
Tel: (525) 211-6243/6308
E-mail:
74174.504@compuserv.com

California
Mexico, D.F.
Tel: (525) 747-8260-67
E-mail:
calmex@mail.internet.com.mx

Colorado
Mexico, D.F.
Tel: (525) 122-2963, 647-5908/9799
E-mail:
75452.1253@compuserve.com

Florida
Mexico, D.F.
Tel: (525) 546-1518/1519/1828
E-mail:
martinexflmx@iserve.net.mx

Georgia
Mexico D.F.
Tel: (525) 207-8011/9836

Idaho
Guadalajara, Jal.
Tel: (523) 121-2158, 647-8000
E-mail:
internet74173.667@compuserve.com

Illinois
Mexico, D.F.
Tel: (525) 747-8190 to 94
E-mail: ilray@ibm.net

Indiana
Mexico, D.F.
Tel: (525) 550-1014, 616/2486/2984
E-mail: indiana@intmex.com

Iowa
Mexico, D.F.
Tel: (525) 536-0561, 682-2458
E-mail:
tallegretti@attmail.com

Louisiana
Mexico, D.F.

Tel: (525) 520-9369
E-mail:
epax@genemp.com.mx

Maryland
Mexico, D.F.
Tel: (525) 514-1769, 525-6807
E-mail: ndeg@ds.uas.mx

Massachusetts
Mexico, D.F.
Tel: (525) 280-9087/9688
E-mail:
cglamex@mail.tesssa.com

Michigan
Mexico, D.F.
Tel: (525) 611-8954/8958
E-mail:
otmanxxx@iserve.net.mx

Minnesota
Mexico, D.F.
Tel: (525) 626-0400 ext. 2026

Missouri
Guadalajara, Jal.
Tel: (523) 616-6251
Email:
rpmiss@foreigner.class.udg.mx

New Mexico
Mexico, D.F.
Tel: (525) 207-7619, 208-1515

North Carolina
Huizquilucan, Edo. de Mexico

Tel: (525) 245-9041/42
E-mail:
74054.1031@compuserve.com

Ohio
Mexico, D.F.
Tel: (525) 525-3132
E-mail:
103226.561@compuserve.com

Pennsylvania
Mexico, D.F.
Tel: (525) 660-0665/0979/1104
E-mail:
procorfi@mail.internet.com.mx

Puerto Rico
Mexico, D.F.
Tel: (525) 282/9175/76

Rhode Island
Mexico, D.F.
Tel: (525) 683-1277

Texas
Mexico, D.F.
Tel: (525) 546-8173, 566-6628

Utah State
Mexico, D.F.
Tel: (525) 525-5606/5706

Wisconsin
Mexico, D.F.
Tel: (525) 533-0573/4745/
6217
E-mail: wtom@data.net.mx

LANGUAGE SCHOOLS

Most language schools in Mexico offer classes that are individually tailored. The student works one-on-one with a tutor and may join some group sessions. Most language schools offer placement with local families.

CUERNAVACA

The following are some of Cernavaca's most prominent language schools. If you are calling from out of town, first dial the national access (01) code then the city code (73).

Cetlalic Apdo. Postal 1-201, C.P. 62000. Tel 12-6718. Fax 18-0720.

Cuauhnahuac Apdo Postal 5-26, C.P. 62051. Tel. 18-9275. Fax 18-2693

Cuernavaca Language School Apdo. Postal 4-254, C.P. 62430. Tel/Fax 17-5151. or 1409 East Hudson Ave., Salt Lake City, Utah 84106. Tel/Fax (801) 485-8345.

Instituto de Idioma y Cultura en Cuernavaca (formerly IDEAL) Apdo. Postal 2-42, C.P. 62158. Tel. 17-0455, Fax 17-5710.

Instituto de Lengua y Estudios Latinoamericanos Apdo. Postal 2-3 Tel/Fax 17-5294.

The Center for Bilingual Multicultural Studies Apdo. Postal 1520, C.P. 62000. Tel 14-2488.

GUADALAJARA

Guadalajara Autonomous University's International Language Center (Centro Internacional de Idiomas) For more information call 641-7051, ext. 2251.

GUANAJUATO

Universidad de Guanajuato, Departamento de Servicios al Estudiante, Lascurain de Retana 5, 36000 Guanajuato, Gto. Tel. (473) 2-2770. Fax 2-0278.

SAN MIGUEL DE ALLENDE

Instituto de Allende P.O. Box #85-A, San Miguel de Allende, Gto. Mexico 37700. Tel (01152) 418-2-01-90, Fax (01152) 418-2-45-38. E-mail allende@celaya.ugto.mx. Web site: http://www.ugto.mx/info_turi_gto/sma/allende/new.html

CONVERSION CHART

Length, Distance, Area	Multiply by
inches to centimeters	2.54
centimeters to inches	0.39
feet to meters	0.30
meters to feet	3.28
yards to meters	0.91
meters to yards	1.09
miles to kilometers	1.61
kilometers to miles	0.62
acres to hectares	0.40
hectares to acres	2.47

Weight	Multiply by
ounces to grams	28.35
grams to ounces	0.035
pounds to kilograms	0.45
kilograms to pounds	2.21
British tons to kilograms	1016
U.S. tons to kilograms	907

Volume	Multiply by
imperial gallons to liters	4.55
liters to imperial gallons	0.22
U.S. gallons to liters	3.79
liters to U.S. gallons	0.26

A liter is slightly more than a U.S. quart

Temperature

Centigrade to Fahrenheit: Multiply by 1.8 and add 32
Fahrenheit to Centigrade: Subtract 32 and multiply by .56

MEET AN OVERSEAS ENTREPRENEUR

Creator and director of the Living and Making Money Series, Robert Lawrence Johnston III was a vice president with CB Commercial Real Estate Company in California before moving to Costa Rica in 1992.

Taking his own advise, he started a business "offshore" in Costa Rica to take advantage of the region's low cost-of-living, perfect climate and growing business opportunities, without the taxes and over-regulation of back home.

Johnston's first overseas ventures, some successful, some not, included two real estate magazines, a pocket-sized language book, and a "lifestyles" bus tour.

His first Living and Making Money book was published in

1992 in response to the many foreigners, like himself, moving to Costa Rica needing help with everything from opening a bank account to investing in real estate. A few years, hundreds of interviews and a bunch of rubber shoe soles later, he completed his second book, *Living and Making Money in Central America* and then his third, *Living and Making Money in Mexico*.

His books have helped hundreds of U.S. and Canadian citizens take the step across the border into foreign lands. Many of these now seasoned expatriates have prospered in business. But even more important, many have discovered new ways to measure quality of life, by appreciating different cultures and enjoying life on simpler terms — uncomplicated and rewarding.

Johnston now divides his time between administering his "Living Overseas" seminars in the U.S., and updating and investigating abroad business opportunities for his book series.

With computers, faxes, the Internet, overnight mail, cellular phones and daily flights to and from the U.S., more and more people are finding it easier to benefit from the opportunities in emerging markets...

...And don't forget Uncle Sam's gift to U.S. expatriates: Totally tax-free income up to $72,000.